The Winner's Guide to Fantasy Baseball

By

Chris Lee

authorHOUSE™

1663 LIBERTY DRIVE, SUITE 200
BLOOMINGTON, INDIANA 47403
(800) 839-8640
WWW.AUTHORHOUSE.COM

First published by AuthorHouse 02/22/05

ISBN: 1-4208-1969-0 (sc)

Printed in the United States of America
Bloomington, Indiana

This book is printed on acid-free paper.

Table of Contents

This book is dedicated to my parents, and especially my father, for taking me to countless baseball games as a child, picking up all the baseball cards I left around the house, and putting up with more hours of my watching Braves and Cubs games than I could ever count. This book would not have been possible without your love and encouragement. I love you both.

Batting Practice

An introduction to the topic, the author, and the book

My introduction to fantasy baseball took place in 1986 -- for me, half a lifetime ago (I was a freshman in high school that year). Everyone in the neighborhood knew I was a baseball nut, so one day Chuck McKinney -- the father of a friend down the block -- handed me a book about something called "Rotisserie Baseball" ™. He wanted to know what players he should draft for his team and asked for my advice. I'd never heard of it, but as I leafed through the book I was immediately hooked on the game. Weeks later, his league needed another owner for a ten-team league, so Chuck asked me to co-own a team with his son, James. He even paid the fee, provided we pay him back from our winnings, if any. We were intimidated by the prospect of competing with men twice our age, but joined anyway. With a little luck in the season's last week we managed to finish third. Within two years, James's interest had shifted towards music -- and sadly, Chuck died of a heart attack five years later -- but I haven't missed a season since.

In 1986, I did not know a single person outside our league who had heard of fantasy baseball. Now there are TV and radio shows and magazines about fantasy baseball, internet sites that tell how Cliff Floyd's trade to the Expos five minutes ago will effect his fantasy owners, and even 900 numbers for owners who feel the need to know about Larry Walker's latest hangnail before anyone else. Fantasy baseball has helped keep Major League Baseball alive through strikes, lockouts, and drug scandals. In times where free agency has so changed MLB that it's harder than ever to maintain loyalty to a particular team, fantasy baseball makes the game fun. Now, it's estimated that five million people play some form of fantasy baseball. Even casual fans that don't have a fantasy team are somewhat familiar with the game.

About me, and how I can help you

I write this book as someone who can identify with most of you reading it with perhaps one notable exception -- I've played the game longer than most of you, and perhaps longer than some of you have been alive. I've won a few leagues and finished "in the money" more times than I can count. But perhaps more importantly, I've made a lot of mistakes that taught me valuable lessons which I'll share in the following pages.

The most successful major-league baseball managers realize there is both an art and science to managing. This is also true of good fantasy baseball owners. Much of this book deals with statistics and dollar values and what to make of them. They're vital to your success. But unless you play against robots or Lloyd McClendon, there are elements of strategy and psychology as well. Owners commonly make mistakes that fit into one of two categories: A) Trusting their numbers and operating as if in a vacuum, ignoring common sense, gut feelings, and actions or feelings of fellow owners; or, B) Disregarding the math and playing totally on intuition and emotion. Having erred on both sides, I strongly encourage you to read *all* of what I say in a particular chapter. If you're a number-cruncher, heed my warnings when I tell you that sometimes the math should take a back-seat to common sense. If you're mathematically-challenged, don't just glance at the spreadsheet formulas and assume they're beyond your comprehension -- you *will* learn how to compute meaningful dollar values for your league.

I've never played a year of fantasy baseball without learning at least one important lesson. Whether you're new to this game or have played for twenty years, there's something here for everyone.

Purpose of the book

I didn't write this book to tell you there's always a right or wrong way to do everything, or to tell you that Carlos Beltran will be worth $42 in 2005. Instead, my work is meant as a teaching tool, a guide to give you basic principles and to teach you to think for yourself. If you pick up this book and all the players I speak of are no longer active in baseball or the rules in my leagues are different from yours, it doesn't mean the book is irrelevant to you.

In short, this book is for you if:

- *You play in most fantasy or Rotisserie-style leagues.*

- *You're open to new ideas on how to improve your team and your skills as an owner.*

- *You don't mind spending extra time to get an edge over your competitors.*

However, this book is probably not for you if:

- *You play in a simulation-type league where you play games against other opponents and your role mirrors that of an actual major-league manager.*

- *You want this book to be a "magic potion" by which you have to do no further work on your own after reading it.*

- *You're a cynic who believes there's nothing new you can learn about winning at fantasy baseball.* While I do believe that there's something to learn here for even the most experienced players, you probably won't be any better by reading the book if you're convinced you know it all.

Finally, a few words for those of you who might be reluctant to read this book for various reasons:

- *"This book's content is way over my head."* My goal was to write a book so that even a teenager with limited baseball knowledge can comprehend the material. The content may appear overwhelming at first, but I've broken large concepts into smaller steps so that each person can learn at his own pace.

- *"This book has a lot of math, and I'm horrible with numbers."* Relax! I've explained even the most complex of calculations in simple steps.

- *"I've never used a spreadsheet."* You can use this book without ever touching a computer if you wish, though that's neither ideal nor efficient. Before you know it, you'll be able to build a working value system and understand the underlying process.

The Winner's Guide to Fantasy Baseball is your roadmap to success for all aspects of fantasy baseball. You'll learn about key information sources, scouting players, drafting and trading and off-season roster management. You'll learn basic principles you can still use to value players in 2013 or make a good trade in 2005. Read and enjoy, and if you have feedback or constructive criticism, feel free to contact me at chris@baseballhandbook. com. I'm always listening and looking for ways to improve on what I've written.

Book overview

I've divided this book into topics (or "innings") that make navigation as easy as possible. Most every chapter within the book relates to the other chapters in some way. The book generally builds upon itself, so if you skip ahead, you could very well miss key pieces of information. I've done my best to make the book flow both logically and chronologically -- from the first things you need to do (find good sources of information) to the last (in-season roster management).

Inning One, "Doing your homework" (or chapter one, if you prefer), shows how to find the best fantasy baseball information on the newsstands, the Internet and elsewhere. Once you're adequately armed and dangerous, you'll learn how to evaluate players (Inning Two: "Evaluating players and forecasting their performance") and make accurate predictions of the statistics they'll generate in the future.

The next logical step is to assign value to those players based on the stats you've projected, but first you'll need to know a few things about your league. In Inning Three, "Standings points," you'll step away from those players and their statistics momentarily to learn how each league's dynamics and owner personalities influence player value. Here, I'll show you how to calculate some critical numbers that form the basis of your player value system. Before the end of the chapter, I'll refer back to the player pool where you will calculate a "standings point" value for every player in your draft pool. This will be the main determinant of each player's value.

Inning Four, "Player values," takes a brief detour from the player universe to explore how league-specific roster requirements and owner preferences influence player value. Here, I'll introduce some new theories on value determination that I strongly believe are an improvement over traditional practices within the fantasy community. I'll then show you how a player's position may affect his value and then, for those of you who play in auction-style leagues, I'll show you how to generate accurate dollar values for players.

The next segment, "Inflation and dollar values," applies to owners who play in auction leagues where players may be kept from the previous year. You'll discover how each team's keeper list and the prices at which those players were kept influence draft values and how to adjust player salaries accordingly. "The draft" moves from the technical aspects of value and into the psychological realm of draft day. Here you will find tips for outsmarting your competitors at the draft.

The "Seventh-Inning Stretch" covers a hodgepodge of topics that didn't fit elsewhere. Hopefully you'll find some helpful suggestions for your league's rulebook. This chapter also contains as a brief review of stat services and some tips on how to have more fun playing the game.

The next two chapters, "The season," and "Trading," offer pointers on managing your team once the draft is completed. Finally, "The minor leagues" shows how to evaluate players who have not yet reached the majors.

First Inning

Doing your homework

When I joined the Elm Hill Pikers' League (now known as the Granny White Pikers' League), Randy Fletcher dominated the competition. He won eight championships -- most of them by a large margin -- and just missed two more by the respective margins of one save and one hit. Randy dominated for a couple of reasons: he was very intelligent, and he had better information than the rest of us. Randy had practically memorized everything Bill James had ever written, while the rest of us didn't know Bill James from Rick James. By way of his wisdom and outstanding information, Randy was at the top of the standings every October.

But shortly after the dawn of the Internet age, Randy became mortal. He no longer won the league every year -- in fact, he even finished out of the money once or twice. Now, everyone else's information was on par with Randy's. Simply finishing in the top half of the league was evidently no longer fun for a man who was accustomed to winning every season. Eventually, he lost interest and quit the league.

This story illustrates the biggest difference between fantasy baseball now and ten years ago. The quantity of information available to owners today is exponentially greater than it was around 1990. The three biggest reasons for this are:

1. The Internet. Up-to-the-minute information is now available to anyone via the Internet. Ten years ago, I remember looking forward to seeing the stats published in *USA Today* once a week -- in fact, this was the basis of our weekly standings report. Besides the weekly statistics, information was mostly limited to small blurbs in newspapers, transaction reports, and box scores. Those who had cable TV probably saw most Braves and Cubs games -- if they were lucky, maybe the Mets and Yankees as well -- plus the weekly game or two on the major networks.

Owners who didn't play fantasy baseball until after the mid-1990's probably take timely information for granted. I still remember accessing the Internet for the first time in 1992. To my amazement, I could actually find box scores that were available only moments after a game's completion. There were up-to-date player statistics and message boards where I could correspond with other fantasy owners. Today, this is the norm; some owners might even be upset with a two-minute lag between real-time results and the 'net.

2. The growth of fantasy baseball. I remember trying to explain the concept of fantasy baseball to hard-core MLB fans that'd never heard of our beloved pastime as late as the early-1990's. Now, nearly every avid baseball fan either plays or has played fantasy baseball, or at the very least is vaguely familiar with the game. Because of the hobby's explosion in the past decade, we now have dozens of ways to follow the game: fantasy baseball preview issues on newsstands, regular fantasy baseball columns in *Sports Weekly* and *The Sporting News,* even radio and television shows on fantasy baseball. Fantasy owners weren't always this blessed with abundant and timely information.

3. Cable and satellite television. If anything significant happens in a game, the world sees it immediately. If a rookie reels off a couple of impressive starts, he becomes a household name in the baseball world in a matter of weeks. (Dontrelle Willis, anyone?) Once upon a time, some MLB team would make the annual August deal to acquire Todd Zeile for a single-A prospect, and that player's name was nothing more than a footnote in the papers the following day. Now, cable television shows such as *ESPN's Baseball Tonight* tell us everything about the player but his jock size within minutes of the trade.

The information avalanche is only picking up speed, and as a result the races are closer than ever in the two leagues in which I play. Yesterday's cellar-dwelling owner is now tomorrow's pennant contender. The sheer volume of information levels the playing field, which means owners must work harder than ever to gain an advantage on their competitors.

However, all information is not necessarily good information, and to win, you must sort the good from the bad. This takes a considerable amount of time, so I've done of the lot of the weeding for you.

About the ratings

Each source is rated from one to five stars on its usefulness to *fantasy owners*, not on its merit as a whole. Most are quality publications or websites, but their value to a fantasy owner varies widely. If a site or publication is rated below three stars, it's probably not worth purchasing or viewing. If something's rated three stars, I'm neutral on whether you should buy or use it -- it may have one really unique feature or it could be a good comprehensive site that's not particularly-distinguishable from the rest. Anything rated three-and-a-half stars or higher is worth a look. It's important that you read the reasons behind the ratings -- something that's not useful to one owner could be immensely valuable because of a particular feature or because many leagues differ in rules, composition, and scoring methods.

Anyway, here's a comprehensive review of places to go for fantasy information. To help you differentiate among them, I've included the costs, pros, cons and unique features associated with each source rated three stars or above. Most prices listed have been updated through 2004.

Annual publications

Many excellent books and magazines on fantasy baseball are published annually. Most offer a large amount of information in a portable form and are usually a good value for the amount of information you get. The downside is that too much of the content, other than historical statistics and data like player height and weight, is often obsolete by the time the book or magazine is published. Even so, it's hard to win without buying at least one or two of these publications every year.

Street and Smith's Baseball Yearbook ($6.99)

Two stars

Street and Smith's has perhaps been in print longer than Don Zimmer's been in baseball. It's a good read for the general baseball fan but just not much use to fantasy owners. In recent years, the editors have added a small fantasy guide, but it is only minimally helpful for serious owners. It contains some useful information, such as MLB 40-man rosters complete with last year's statistics, but not enough to justify purchase for fantasy purposes alone.

Pros: Entertaining read, collectible due to long history
Cons: Written for baseball fans and not necessarily for fantasy players

Unique features: None

Who's Who in Baseball ($9.95)

Two stars

Who's Who in Baseball published their 89th edition in 2004, and absolutely nothing has changed from past issues. It is simply an alphabetized record, separated by hitters and pitchers, of the career stats of all significant, active MLB players. The pages read like the back of a baseball card. It's useful as a reference guide, but the downside is that it does not include many marginal players or promising rookies.

If you need a reference book, you're probably better off purchasing one of *Baseball America* or *The Sporting News'* publications as they have a better player selection. However, the one thing I like about *Who's Who* is their comprehensive listing of a player's transaction record, including trades, releases, and stays on the disabled list (DL). Unfortunately, DL transactions only list the dates the player was injured and do not tell you the nature of the injury.

Pros: Lots of stats in portable format, DL histories
Cons: Doesn't include stats on enough players, DL histories don't discuss the nature of the injuries
Unique features: DL transactions

The Sporting News Fantasy Baseball ($7.99)

Three stars

The Sporting News' Fantasy Baseball guide offers a large volume of information for a magazine. It includes a brief capsule of over 1,000 players with statistics for each player's previous three years and a three-year average of those statistics, and there are the usual position-eligibility charts as well. There are player groupings into categories such as "sleeper picks," "flukes," even players deemed to be "on the rise" or "primed for career years." Other standard features of most magazines -- prospect ratings, player rankings, projected batting orders and pitching rotations, and injury analysis -- are also present. One particularly-helpful feature is a chart measuring "park effects" which compare the respective batting averages and home runs hit within each park. The magazine's editors solicit input from over a dozen writers, so readers get a wide variety of opinions. There is an extensive list of dollar values too, but these have limited use for reasons I'll discuss in the valuation chapters. Another downfall is that the publication goes to press in mid-December; so much of the content is irrelevant by draft day.

Pros: Lots of info -- good bang for the buck, variety of writers and opinions
Cons: Goes to press in December, no predictions -- only historical stats and averages
Unique features: Park effects chart

Lindy's Fantasy Baseball ($6.99)

Three and one-half stars

Lindy's, long a major publisher of college and professional sports preview issues, has just recently entered the fantasy sports market. Their debut has been impressive, and I really like *Lindy's* layout, which includes lots of color pictures and an easily-readable format.

Player profiles are detailed and include previous season's statistics in on-base and slugging percentages, batting averages versus left and right-handed pitching, and at-bats per home run. The player selection is adequate -- perhaps not as deep as other publications -- but good enough for most leagues. Their "draft checklist" is helpful to owners wishing to take just one magazine to their draft.

I was fairly impressed with their position breakdowns -- included are "rising," "falling," "underrated," "sleeper," "super sleeper," "risky business," and "value play" candidates at each spot on the diamond as well as the "best power" and "best base stealer" at each offensive slot. For pitchers, there's an extensive snapshot of each team's bullpen including closers and "closers in waiting." *Lindy's* also provides a deep list of minor league prospects at each position, including the magazine's best guesses at which players will eventually become stars.

Pros: Impressive debut effort, and they hit big with a couple of their very short list of sleeper picks for 2004 (namely Ben Sheets and Craig Wilson); player projections are also nice
Cons: Though most players you'll need to know about are profiled, they'll still miss a few guys that those of you in ultra-deep, AL or NL-only leagues might need to know about
Unique features: None to speak of, though most magazines don't offer the sheer number of projections that *Lindy's* does

Chris Lee

Major League Baseball Yearbook ($8.95)
Three and one-half stars

The *Major League Baseball Yearbook* is the most expensive of all the magazines I've seen, but also contains more information (150,000 words, 50,000 stats) than most. There's a two-page summary on each team, complete with projected batting orders and pitching rotations which usually are out-of-date by the end of the spring. *MLB Yearbook* profiles approximately 480 players, including two years of player statistics of both pre and post-All-Star game performances for each player. *MLB Yearbook* also features two pages of profiles per position which includes the top ten minor league players at each.

The writers, while entertaining, seem to value their own opinions above common sense at times. Consider this statement from the 2003 edition -- "Marcus Giles is just not good at baseball" – in spite of Giles' two minor-league MVP awards and severe injury problems that were solely responsible for a sub-par 2002. Giles promptly had an all-star caliber season in 2003 -- something a shrewd analyst could have easily foreseen. However, rookie owners who have not developed the knack for player analysis should perhaps look elsewhere.

Pros: A ton of info, entertaining writing, schedules for every team
Cons: Expensive, and the writers' opinions are sometimes more entertaining than accurate
Unique feature: Top 10 prospects at each position -- deepest prospect lists of any magazine

The Sporting News Scouting Notebook (in partnership with Stats, Inc.) ($19.95)
Three and one-half stars

This book contains scouting reports on almost every significant major league player as well as lots of useless information. Included are platoon splits for hitters and pitchers (how each hitter did against left and right-handed pitching, and how each pitcher did against left and right-handed hitters) and charts of where each batter's hits landed. I like the summaries of players' base running abilities and the inclusion of obscure stats such as percentage of stolen-base attempts allowed by pitchers. However, most fantasy owners lack the time to wade through a mountain of information for mostly trivial details.

Pros: Enormous amount of info, obscure stats

6

Cons: Too much to sort through to get to the good stuff, pricey
Unique features: The obscure stats and analysis

Fantasy Baseball Index ($6.99)

Four stars

Led by a reputable staff of writers (Mat Olkin, John Sickels, and Justin Eleff), *FBI* provides the basics one would expect from a fantasy publication, including historical stats from every MLB player who played a game the previous season. There are projected depth charts and statistics, evaluations of top prospects, lists of sleepers and overrated players, and dollar values for 4x4 and 5x5 leagues. *Moneyball* fans, take note -- *FBI* provides OPS stats (on-base plus slugging percentage) for all players. Players are categorized, within their position, based on what the editors expect (Examples include, "Instead of bidding on a washed-up vet, bid $1 on:" and "Look for a breakout year from:"). There's a list of key players from each team to follow in the draft -- usually big-name players who are high-risk, high-reward players -- and the listing of best and worse-case scenarios for each. *FBI* also surveyed five of the "experts" for their answers on dozens of questions ranging from "What NL player is most likely to earn $10 more than he's purchased for in most drafts" to "Who will be the AL Roto MVP in 2005."

Pros: Categorization of players into helpful groups, top-notch analysts
Cons: Not too many, not as in-depth as 4.5 & 5-star books
Unique features: List of young pitchers who may be candidates for arm trouble based on overuse at an early age, experts' lists of answers to Roto questions

Future Stars, by John Benson and Tony Blengino ($19.95)

Four stars

Co-author John Benson has done player analysis and evaluation for many years, and his work, *Future Stars,* is a comprehensive guide to minor leaguers. In the book, Benson rates the best players in every MLB organization and in every minor league. The 2004 edition was 251 pages and included profiles of any player you should want to know about, along with each player's major-league equivalent statistics, or "MLE's" (MLE's are an estimate of what a minor-leaguer would have done at the major-league level, adjusted according to the player's age, level, and home ballpark).

The writing staff features a good-sized network of scouts who see the prospects play in person. Therefore, the book provides information that goes beyond a player's statistical output -- scouting reports of a player's defense, conditioning, athleticism, strengths and weaknesses, and much more. Other key features are the "Relative Production Potential" (hitters) and "Relative Control / Power Potential" (pitchers) which analyze players' statistics in a similar fashion to MLE's. Once these analyses are complete, *Future Stars* compares prospects to their most-comparable major league players; this is a very risky exercise, but nonetheless, it is interesting.

One caution: Several readers who purchased *Future Stars* through Amazon.com received the 2004 edition well after draft day, and many never received it. You may wish to check your local bookstore before purchasing it online.

Pros: No future prospect will go unmentioned here
Cons: Too expensive and comprehensive unless you play in a deep keeper league with minor league drafts, not enough raw stats for the dollar
Unique features: Minor-league depth charts, draft analysis of MLB organizations, Relative Potential analysis

Baseball America's Prospect Handbook ($21.95)
Four stars

Baseball America has focused on the minor leagues and college baseball longer than any other publication, and few can match the volume of information they offer on the minor leagues. *BA's Prospect Handbook* features 900 scouting reports including the top 30 prospects within each organization. Plus, four experts (Alan Simpson, Will Lingo, Jim Callis, and Josh Boyd) each name their top 50 prospects in the minors. There's also a list of the top 100 prospects eligible for the coming year's amateur draft. *BA* also provides fielding stats, which can shed insight as to whether a prospect can field well enough to land an MLB job.

Pros: Most raw data about minor league players
Cons: Expensive and very specialized, no projected future stats, no major-league equivalent stats, players are evaluated as to their value in "real baseball," not fantasy baseball
Unique features: Deepest prospect list for each organization

The Fantasy Baseball Guide (formerly known as "Rotowire's Fantasy Baseball") ($6.99)

Four stars

A very nice magazine for the money. *Fantasy Baseball Guide* offers information on a lot of players -- over 1,600 in 2004 -- which is helpful to those owners playing in leagues with extensive player pools. Each player's stats for the last three years are listed along with a projection for the coming year and a few sentences about that player. Other nice features include position eligibility charts and short essays on draft strategy by some well-known fantasy baseball writers. A great read for anyone, especially those of you on a tight budget.

Pros: Perhaps the best magazine for the money; there's a ton of information and analysis from guys who know what they're doing
Cons: Not as in-depth as the four-and-a-half and five-star books
Unique feature: Stolen bases and stolen-base attempts

The Sporting News Baseball Guide (in partnership with Stats, Inc.) ($17.95)

Four stars

This handy book featuring stats for every major and minor-league player from the previous year, including fielding stats. It features spring rosters, league leaders from the previous year, games played by position for each player, and dimensions of each major league park. There's little from the previous year that's not contained in this book.

Pros: A comprehensive reference guide in one place
Cons: No player projections or data from years beyond last season
Unique features: Ballpark dimensions

The Baseball Prospectus ($21.95)

Four and one-half stars

The *Prospectus* is great source, offering in-depth coverage of about 1,600 players each year. If a prospect has major-league experience or has even a glimmer of hope at being in The Show one day, he's probably in the book. The *Prospectus* is unique in that, instead of just giving a player's stats, they normalize all leagues and parks so each player's stats are in what they call a "ballpark neutral" environment. They also adjust player stats according to their levels of minor-league experience.

Perhaps the best part of the book is the organizational capsules and comments for each player. They make for interesting reading, and give you some hard-to-find information on prospects. For $21.95 (you may find it cheaper on-line), it's probably worth the price for serious players.

Pros: Outstanding and entertaining analysis, editors really do their homework on any player of significance
Cons: No actual stats, only "normalized" ones, so plan on investing in one other publication to get those
Unique features: The folks at *The Prospectus* spend several pages analyzing each organization and their management philosophy as a whole. This is not something often seen, and certainly not to the extent that *The Prospectus* does this.

Baseball Forecaster, by Ron Shandler ($23.95)
Five stars

I highly recommend Ron *Shandler's Baseball Forecaster* -- it provides readers with a wealth of historical values and projections for the coming year. Shandler's approach to forecasting is very different from most of the fantasy writers. He sees predicting a player's exact statistics as an exercise in futility for a number of reasons, but mostly because those stats largely determined by things beyond his control. For instance, a pitcher's win total is greatly affected by the defense behind him and his team's ability to score runs; likewise, a hitter's RBI stats are a product of playing time, his slot in the batting order and the number and speed of the runners on base when he gets a hit.

Because of these things, Shandler opines that we cannot accurately and consistently predict how many RBI Magglio Ordonez will have or how many games Mark Mulder will win. However, Shandler believes a player's skill level can be easily discerned, and once those skills are taken in context with the player's age, developmental trends, and home ballpark, he can make a better guess at future performance. At the crux of Shandler's thinking is this idea: we cannot ultimately predict a player's exact stats from one year to the next, but all other things being equal, good players will eventually produce good numbers and mediocre player will produce poor statistics.

As a result, *The Forecaster* has computed formulas for almost every aspect of offensive and pitching skill that a fantasy owner would find useful. Formulas for power skills and the player's percentage of fly balls hit are used as a basis for home runs forecasts. Batters are also evaluated by complex formulas for their speed skills and their ability to make contact. Pitchers are judged for their ability to strike out hitters and avoid walks and home runs. These formulas are incorporated into numbers that compare each player to a benchmark that represents "average skill" in each particular area. Finally, Shandler uses these skills evaluations to project a player's stat line for the coming season.

There are several other features of the *Forecaster* that can be useful. For instance, the publication tracks all starting pitcher outings and rates each on a five-point scale so that a pitcher's consistency can be tracked throughout the previous year. Minor-league coverage is excellent as well -- there are MLE's (major-league equivalent stats) for most every player with AA experience or higher, and Shandler also provides a list for each of the top 25 pitching and hitting prospects for the coming year.

Pros: Best source of info in one place, free access on website to updated projections beginning the first of March, humorous at times
Cons: Most expensive of all books, and in the past, Shandler has clung to the worth of his formulas even when certain players consistently defied his predictions. Even so, Shandler continually improves his product and learns to better deal with the statistical outliers with each passing season.
Unique features: Many obscure stats and formulas that offer deeper insight than you'll find anywhere else, and the hands-down best listing of MLE's

Fantasy Baseball Insider ($25)
Not rated

I've never seen a copy but thought you might want to be aware of it in case you wanted to check it out on your own. It's written by the staff at the *Sandlot Shrink* website. They describe their 2003 edition as follows: "180 pages of scouting reports, stat scans, projections and dollar values, strategy essays, and minor-league rankings. 800 players are professionally scouted along with 300 minor leaguers." It's not available in stores, so order by visiting *sandlotshrink.com* or calling 1-440-543-6949. Postage is an additional $1.

Periodicals

There aren't nearly as many good periodicals for fantasy baseball owners are there are annual publications. I haven't even bothered to rate most sport magazines such as *Sports Illustrated* and *ESPN The Magazine* because the fantasy-specific content is so scarce that they don't justify the cost of subscribing if that's what you're after. Here are the best of the periodicals for fantasy baseball players:

The Sporting News **($19.95 for six months)**
Three and one-half stars

TSN was once known as "the Bible for baseball fans." With the proliferation of websites and publications suited for fantasy players, it no longer deserves that title, but it's still a good read. During the season, they devote about 15 pages a week to baseball, including four pages of nothing but reviews for every team. They devote a little coverage to prospects and have a weekly page devoted to fantasy baseball as well.

Pros: Excellent team coverage, weekly fantasy page
Cons: No stats
Unique features: Beat writers from each Major League city

Baseball America **($61.95 for one year)**
Four stars

Baseball America has been around seemingly forever, and does a better job covering the minor leagues and college baseball than anyone else. I recommend *BA* if you play in a super-serious league where you have a deep minor-league or reserve draft. One of the best things about getting the magazine is that you also have access to features on their website, including up-to-date minor league statistics as well their top 15 prospects for each organization.

Pros: Best source for comprehensive minor-league stats and coverage
Cons: Costly and very little MLB info focuses almost exclusively on college and minors
Unique features: Great college baseball coverage, for those of you who like to follow prospects before they enter MLB farm systems

Sports Weekly **($39.95 for one year, $69.90 for two years, $1.50 per single copy)**
Four stars

This publication, formerly known as *Baseball Weekly,* has been around for more than a decade now. Each week, readers get a recap on every MLB team plus stats and the league schedule for the coming weeks. One of the most useful features for fantasy players is comprehensive stats, for both the year and previous week as well as position eligibility data. John Hunt also writes a good weekly column on fantasy baseball, including a list of players who have increased or decreased in value during the last week.

The prospect issues, published each year around December and January, are well worth the money ($1.50 each) and if you don't subscribe, I highly recommend picking up copies. One caveat: *Sports Weekly* began covering football in 2002, so the baseball content has been reduced somewhat.

Pros: Excellent overall coverage, expanded stats, Hunt's column, and their NFL coverage are a great bonus if you play fantasy football.
Cons: Football coverage has impacted space devoted to baseball (no box scores anymore), and because so many people read it, any advantage you gain may be negated
Unique feature: Good minor-league coverage, weekly updates for each organization's statistical leaders at the minor-league level

Websites

Al Gore's Internet is a wonderful invention, but the drawback is that any idiot with a computer can proclaim himself a fantasy baseball expert and start his own site. Therefore it should come as no surprise that much of the fantasy information on the Internet is a waste of time and bandwidth. If you're a veteran player, you can quickly figure out who knows what they're talking about and who doesn't; if you're new to the game, it may not be so easy. If you're a rookie, you would be wise to stick to the sites I review below until you feel comfortable in your ability to separate the good sites from the garbage.

There are dozens of decent fantasy baseball sites in cyberspace. Most offer virtually the same information as their competitors and so I've chosen not to review most of the ones that aren't well-known or that don't offer truly unique features. I would recommend that you add any sites rated "four stars" or higher to your list of Internet bookmarks. At the bottom of the list, I've added a few more sites that didn't quite make the cut but might be worth a look.

Major League Baseball (Free)
mlb.com
Three stars
There are some good fantasy columnists on this site, but in typical MLB fashion, there is little offered here for fantasy baseball players that

you can't find elsewhere. Oh yes, for the low, low price of $14.95 per year, you too can hear live broadcasts of MLB games, which used to be free until Bug Selig found another way to milk the fans' wallets. I'll pass.

Pros: Affiliation with MLB means the occasional story or nugget not found elsewhere
Cons: Not as timely in reporting transactions as other sites
Unique features: Links to all 30 MLB teams' official sites

John Skilton's Baseball Links (Free)

www.baseball-links.com
Three stars

Skilton bills his site as "the most comprehensive collection of links to baseball resources." I doubt anyone is disputing that claim, as he has links to over 10,000 baseball sites, including a section of fantasy and Rotisserie Baseball ™ links, which are updated quite often. I recommend checking the site every few months to see any new resources on the Internet that may be of use. It's a great site for baseball fans in general.

Pros: Site has longevity and links to anything you'd want to find
Cons: 10,000-plus links means some dead and many useless ones
Unique features: Saves you a trip to the search engine

Japanese Baseball (Free)

japanesebaseball.com
Three stars

This site is totally devoted to Japanese baseball, and you can get career stats for any player currently in Japan. They also have a message board which often contains rumors of which players might be heading to the U.S. in future years.

Pros: Rumor mill, Japanese stats (in English)
Cons: Japanese baseball is a different mindset, this site has that and it has limited concern for fantasy owners
Unique features: Find the next Ichiro here

Sandlot Shrink (Some free features, full subscriptions- $89 per year)

Sandlotshrink.com
Free portion: three stars
Paid service: not rated

The Sandlot Shrink, run by John Coleman, Dennis LePore, and USA Today columnist Rod Beaton (among others) includes both a free and a paid section. The subscription (I've never subscribed) contains "daily injury reports, rankings, projections, dollar values, transactions, minor-league call-ups, role changes, trends, pertinent information, news, and notes." As of summer 2004, year-round access is $89, but you may also purchase access from only April to September for $59 or from spring training through April for $39. The web site advertises that they update their site several times per day. They also advertise an "ask the experts" feature in which subscribers may submit pertinent questions to their panel of fantasy baseball gurus.

The free section includes depth charts (which can be very useful around draft day), tips on draft and in-season strategy, and a historical on-line database that allows you to find information for past and present players.

As I've never accessed their paid features, I'm not qualified to rate their paid service. However, their free information is very useful and up to date, and their staff boasts many people who are well-known in fantasy circles, so if it's as good as the free stuff, it's probably worth the price. They also offer similar services for football and basketball.

Pros and Cons not rated -- author does not subscribe
Unique feature: Their free depth charts feature, which I've added to my computer's "favorites" menu

The Baseball Cube

TheBaseballCube.com
Three and one-half stars

It's not a very well-known site, but you will surely want to bookmark this one. It's one of the best sources for career stats of active (and inactive) players because it includes not only major-league stats, but a player's minor-league and college numbers as well. The site's very flexible, as you can search by player as well as browse stats for major and minor-league teams by year and even for some college teams if you wish.

Another really cool feature is the amateur draft lists from every year of the draft's history. You can see the order in which players were selected for every college draft and click on a profile of each player (which, of course, comes complete with statistics).

Pros: Most statistical sites give you complete records of players but don't go back into the minor leagues, and definitely not to college. This site is an absolute must if your leagues require you to know about minor-league and college players.
Cons: Advertising-heavy, and very slow at times. Not much on info and analysis -- the site is what it is, but they do the things they do very well.
Unique features: Where else can you find college stats, complete listings of amateur drafts, or college rosters online? Also, they list caught-stealings, which can be difficult to find.

CBS Sportsline and Commissioner.com (Free, except for stat service)
sportsline.com, commissioner.com
Four stars

CBS Sportsline provides most of the major features the other major players do -- stats, updates, advice, etc. The content and services have greatly improved of late, and if they continue to improve at this rate, they may eventually challenge Rotoworld for the top spot. They do offer a decent stat service for about ten bucks a team -- I find it a little slow and not so user-friendly at times, but it's a good deal for the price. There are several writers devoted exclusively to fantasy baseball, and each has a weekly column devoted to one aspect of the game (e.g. -- "The Wind-Up," a pitching column).

Pros: Site and stat service improves each year, great features for dollars spent on stat service
Cons: Missing some of the essential features, such as minor-league coverage and regular updates of minor-league top prospects. Comprehensive coverage means switching back and forth from stat-service site to sportsline.com
Unique features: Ability to search stats within a date range on stat service, custom reporting features on stat service

ESPN (Mostly free, "Insider" access is $4.95 per month)
espn.com
Four stars

ESPN has the usual transactions, stats, and all the things most other sites have, but what I most like about this site are the columnists -- namely

John Sickels, Joe Morgan, Peter Gammons, and (my favorite) Rob Neyer. Most of the columns are not specifically written for fantasy players (though they do have a fantasy-specific columnist in Brandon Funston) but they're almost always enjoyable and sometimes humorous as well. Sickels is one of the best minor-league analysts in the game and is recommended reading for those of you follow the minors. Fantasy matters aside, I recommend the site for the entertainment alone.

ESPN also offers "insider" access for $39.95 per year or $4.95 per month, and I have noticed that some time between 2003 and 2004, much of what was formerly free is now only available to paid subscribers. Much of their premium service contains nice information -- including trade rumors and other things, and now Neyer's writings. At one time it was not worth the subscription price, but now that ESPN is making most of their good pieces into paid content -- and improving that content markedly -- paying the monthly fee could be a wise investment. I expect that trend will eventually expand to Sickels' work as well. *Disclaimer:* I once did some writing for *ESPN's Insider* features, though it was not fantasy-baseball related.

Pros: Comprehensive site, sortable stats, and excellent writers
Cons: Not as fantasy-oriented as other sites
Unique features: In-depth prospect analysis by Sickels

USA Today Online (Free)

www.usatoday.com/sports/baseball/front.htm
Four and one-half stars

This site has almost everything you need in the way of transactions, box scores, stats, prospect reports, team updates, etc. *USA Today Online* deserves high marks for offering minor-league stats for all teams as well as flexibility in their presentation of major-league stats (you can see stats for the last seven days, last 21 days, and also see a list of all players who homered, won or saved games, or had two or more RBI for the day, among other things). Also, their position eligibility charts are updated throughout the week. To access most of these features, simply click on their "fantasy" link.

There are several good columnists at this site including Paul White, Mat Olkin, and John Hunt. Many of *Sports Weekly's* columns and features are duplicated on this site.

Pros: Tons of stats and knowledgeable writers

Cons: Don't offer depth of player reviews found on some other sites
Unique features: Flexibility in sorting statistics

Fantasy Source Baseball ($19.95 per year)

www.fantasy.sportingnews.com
Four and one-half stars

Like Rotoworld, this site seems to have about everything you'd need. They do an incredible job of covering all the latest baseball news and how the most recent events affect fantasy owners. They have the standard features you'd want in a site (stats, news, injuries, prospect lists, etc.) plus special features such as their lineup tracker and rotation tracker, which allow you to see which players have fallen in or out of favor with MLB managers. Brendan Roberts and Kevin Wheeler offer excellent commentary on the NL and AL, respectively. In short, the site offers everything a fantasy owner needs to stay on top of things. For $6.95, the site offered a "Draft Kit" in 2003, which I've never seen so I won't review it here.

Note: The content I have reviewed here was formerly free -- since I'm not a paid member, I'm assuming the quality level has not decreased, which is probably a good assumption since they seem to have added more features.

Pros: Top notch coverage in every aspect
Cons: It's a pay site; Rotoworld offers similar coverage for free
Unique features: Head-to-head match-ups for hitters vs. the pitchers they'll be facing in coming games, ballparks' effects on statistical outputs

Rotoworld (Free)

Rotoworld.com
Four and one-half stars

A free service affiliated with All Star Stats, Rotoworld has also been in cyberspace for a number of years. If I could use only one website to track breaking news on players, this would be it. Rotoworld's strength is that they provide up-to-date information on any player in baseball from superstars to insignificant benchwarmers and, on occasion, obscure minor-leaguers about whom no one cares, other than their mothers and girlfriends. Their site is updated many times a day, and also provides links to all the hometown papers of each major league club. There is also a useful search feature which allows you to find any player along with recent news about that player, his career statistics dating back to 1990, and the player's statistics for each of the last ten days.

Other helpful features include their list of the top 100 prospects, complete with up-to-date statistics throughout the year, advice columns, depth charts, and player rankings. You'll definitely want to add this site to your Internet bookmarks. As with Sandlot Shrink, they offer similar services for basketball, football, and hockey and also own a stat service (All-Star Stats) that costs around $50 a year per team. For about $15, you may also purchase a draft kit from *Rotoworld*.

Pros: One stop shopping -- if you want to find it, it's likely here, and best of all, it's free!

Cons: Content is good, but player analysis is sometimes suspect and some of the writers need to re-take Freshman Composition. Also, *Rotoworld* mostly re-reports news found elsewhere, so little news is broken here first.

Unique features: Links to hometown newspapers for all teams

Other websites of note

Here are some other notable sites I have chosen not to review in full. Few of these have anything you could not get from any of the sites I listed above. I suspect that several will be dead sites by the time you read this, but perhaps a few will improve their content and bear watching in the future. *Note*: A few of these require paid subscriptions.

AlexPatton.com: Alex Patton is a well-respected writer and stats guru in the fantasy baseball community and you can access his writings and player projections from here.

AskRotoman.com: This appears to be the online companion to *The Fantasy Baseball Guide.* It's poorly laid-out and not nearly as impressive as the magazine.

BaseballAmerica.com (**$42 per year**): The online companion to their magazine.

BaseballGuru.com: The usual stuff -- projections, commentary and message boards, etc. Most features are free, but they also offer a service for a buck a month that delivers the latest player news to your E-mail account. One unique feature is their updates and commentary on American players playing in other countries. It's new to me, but the writers seem competent and it looks like a nice site.

***BaseballHQ.com* ($99 per year):** This is the premium online companion site to *The Forecaster.* If it's up-to-snuff with the publication, (I have not subscribed, but likely will for the coming season) it's worth the price. Shorter-term subscriptions are available at a discount.

BaseballInfoSolutions.com: This one appears to be a good site to visit in case you wish to purchase player statistics from past years and download them to your computer.

BaseballNotebook.com: A free site that follows the day-to-day happenings in baseball and their fantasy implications.

***BaseballProspectus.com* ($39.95 per year):** I have never subscribed as I just recently discovered the site, but I suspect the content is outstanding. Among others, Will Carroll, former publisher of the web site "Under the Knife," which was the best site I'd ever seen in evaluating injuries, is on the staff there. That alone might make a subscription worth the money. And, of course, I'm sure a lot of the same great stuff that is in their book is also online. It's certainly worth a look.

Baseball-Reference.com: One of the best sites for historical stats on any player you'd care to find.

BaseballThinkFactory.com: More of a sight for intelligent baseball thought and discussion than anything, as it's certainly not directed towards the fantasy owner. However, it's always good to stay abreast of recent baseball research and read intelligent commentary on the game -- you can often apply that knowledge and become a better owner.

CreativeSports.com: Another run-of-the-mill site with the same info, analysis, and message boards that dozens of other sites also offer.

FantasyBaseballCafe.com: Provides links to other sites and a message board for fantasy leaguers to exchange ideas. This looks like one of the better sites among those I haven't rated, and seems to have a very active message board community.

FantasyBaseballNews.com: Subscription-based service I've never used; offers news, prospect coverage, and statistical analysis. It's also known as "Fantasy Insights."

Fantistics.com: Another paid service I've never used. They have the usual projections, analysis, and other information of the paid sites.

MastersBall.com ($39.95 **per year):** Another paid service with paid projections, analysis, etc. I haven't used it and just became aware of this before publication time, though they've been around since 1997.

ProspectReport.com: I haven't followed the site long enough to vouch for the credibility of their writers, but they've obviously worked hard. They rate and review over 300 minor-leaguers.

RotoMag.com: Per the statement on their home page, "Rotomagazine is written and produced by two actuaries that honestly have nothing better to do. An Ivy League graduate in Statistics and an Actuarial Science graduate with a Mathematics minor, they have been playing fantasy baseball of one form or another for over 45 years combined, starting with the Strat-O-Matic board game and MicroLeague Baseball on the Commodore 64 as children, but graduating to years of competitive Roto experience." For now this site is new and thin on content, but they did offer their free second-half projections for 2004.

RotoWire.com ($60 **per year):** Formerly known as RotoNews, this website is affiliated with the popular Wall Street Sports site. For $60 a year they offer the same basic services as listed above -- draft prep information, player updates, depth charts, etc. They also offer subscription terms for one, three, or six months, and offer services for basketball, football, and hockey. I've never used their paid services and so I haven't rated them, but they were a free site until 2001. At that time their information was solid.

Television

ESPN's *Baseball Tonight*
Four Stars

Yes, you can get much of the same information on *Baseball Tonight* from the Internet or from reading box scores, but isn't it more fun to actually *watch* highlights of players than read about them? The cast of *Baseball Tonight* changes from year to year -- usually, one of the previous year's hosts gets a job as a major league manager and is replaced by one who was just fired -- but the quality remains excellent from year to year. Regulars among the show's crew include former major-leaguers Joe Morgan and Harold Reynolds. Boston sportswriter Peter Gammons usually offers some good opinions and analysis, especially when it comes to rumors of personnel moves and trades as well as insight on minor-league prospects (He also bears a striking resemblance to Andrew Jackson on the new $20 bill). As with ESPN's website, it's worth viewing for the entertainment value alone.

Pros: It's a very entertaining and insightful show, and you get the chance to see your players' highlights rather than just read about them in the box scores
Cons: Everyone else in your league is probably already watching it, and Morgan and Reynolds come from the "old school" that refuses to recognize the importance of stats like on-base and slugging percentages, so you have to somewhat discount their analysis
Unique features: In addition to Reynolds and Morgan, many of the personalities on the show (Rob Dibble, John Kruk, Jeff Brantley, and in the past, Bobby Valentine, Brian McRae, Mike MacFarlane, and Buck Showalter) are guys who played or managed at the big-league level for a long time

"Cream of the crop"

If you want to save time and stick to using only the very best sources of information, these are the ones I'd recommend. Please note that many of these are websites, so please refer to the previous pages for their Internet addresses.

Best free website for the latest player news: *Rotoworld*

Best free website for current depth charts: *Sandlot Shrink.* I prefer *Sandlot Shrink* over *Rotoworld* because you can view an entire division's depth-charts at a glance, whereas you have to view *Rotoworld's* on a team-by-team basis.

Best free website for a comprehensive log of MLB transactions: *None.* America can put a man on the moon and cure deadly diseases but can't build a website that has a comprehensive MLB transaction record. If you find one, please let me know. Even MLB's official website is deficient in this area. My favorite place to go is ESPN.com, but I also check mlb. com, usatoday.com, cbssportsline.com and foxsports.com. However, they all seem to miss several transactions per month, so you're forced to cross-reference all those sites. Sometimes, they all miss the same transaction. This is particularly annoying when you play in a league that requires proof of a player's removal from a team's active roster in order for his fantasy owner to reserve or release him.

Best free website for in-season minor-league stats: *USA Today* and *Baseball America.* (Much of *BA* is for paid subscribers only, but minor league stats are still free). *The Baseball Cube* is good during the off-season and is improving their in-season coverage, but it appears that they're making their in-season minor league stats a paid feature.

Best place for free information on Japanese players: *japanesebaseball. com*

Best columnists and baseball analysis on the Web: *ESPN.com,* though admittedly this is a little biased because I find their writers to be very entertaining.

Best pre-season projections: *Ron Shandler's Baseball Forecaster*

Best player analysis: *Ron Shandler's Baseball Forecaster,* with an honorable mention to *Baseball Prospectus.*

Second Inning

Evaluating players and forecasting their performance

A big key to success in fantasy baseball success is an owner's ability to evaluate players and know their true value. Proper player evaluation is crucial to drafting, trading, and managing your roster throughout the season. This talent alone generally separates good fantasy owners from average or bad ones. Successful fantasy owners must have the ability to look beyond the performance gauges that most baseball fans use (homers, RBI, ERA, etc.) and instead at other indicators which may be better measures of a player's talent. If you look only at three-year averages or last season's numbers, you could be missing important clues regarding a player's true talent and which direction his career is heading.

Player evaluation is not an exact science. Though the baseball stat gurus have made great strides in the last decade, there will never be foolproof methods to explain past performance or predict a player's future. But if an owner knows a few secrets about player evaluation, his chance of choosing the right players for his team becomes substantially better. In the pages ahead, I'll illustrate some keys to evaluating both hitting and pitching talent.

Evaluating hitters

No matter what statistical categories a league uses, hitters should be evaluated in three areas: their raw talent (such as their ability to hit for average and/or get on base, their ability to hit for power, and their ability on the base paths), "talent-independent" factors such as age, and the external factors that the player can't control. Here's what to look for in each hitter:

Talent factors

"Player-specific factors" are those that relate almost exclusively to a player's God-given ability. They are:

Ability to get on base and hit for average

Batting average is perhaps the most difficult statistic to predict, but here are a few guidelines that may help in evaluating hitters for batting average and on-base potential:

1. *Successful hitters make the most of their plate appearances.* The best hitters usually wait for a good pitch before swinging. This is why Barry Bonds and Todd Helton finish every season among the league walks leaders. Pitchers are forced to throw strikes or walk them. Since hitting a good pitch is easier than hitting a bad one, selective hitters generally have a better chance of hitting for a high average.

2. *Conversely, impatient hitters tend to swing at bad pitches, causing them to strike out more often, walk less, and produce lower batting averages.* Pitchers know they can get undisciplined hitters out without giving them something to hit. Consequently, these hitters probably won't consistently see good pitches. Be especially cautious of young hitters who swing at everything. Young hackers might sustain a good average for a few months or even a year or two, but when pitchers realize they'll swing at anything, these hitters usually see their averages plummet faster than O. J. Simpson's endorsement opportunities in the mid-1990's.

3. *The more a hitter puts the ball in play, the more likely he is to get a hit -- especially if the he's fast.* Brett Butler and Rickey Henderson were classic examples of this -- they'd put the ball in play and use their speed to find a way to get on base. Hitters who consistently make contact are also the beneficiary of more fluke hits -- bad-hop grounders, fly balls that outfielders lose in the sun, etc. There are a lot more seeing-eye singles than strikeout victims who beat the dropped throw on the third strike.

A few hitters, such as Garret Anderson and Vladimir Guerrero, are exceptions to these rules. Anderson, who walks infrequently and strikes out regularly (though he's nowhere near the top of the strikeout leader board), manages to hit for very good averages year-in and year-out because most everything he hits, he hits hard. Guerrero, on the other hand, is a pure freak. He's able to consistently hit pitches wherever they're thrown (sometimes that means pitches a foot out of the strike zone) and usually hit them hard. Players like Guerrero, who has incredible God-given talent, are so rare that there are only a very small handful of them in baseball at any particular time.

However, the norm seems to be players like Derek "Operation Shutdown" Bell and Homer Bush who hack their way to .300 once or twice and are out of a full-time job within a couple of years. (Coming off a .173 campaign in 2001 (plus a .163 month at AAA, for good measure), Bell threatened to go into "operation shutdown" if forced to compete for a job. The Pirates, for once, did something right and released him.) To further prove my point, both players were in the majors when I began writing this book and out of the Big Show by its publication date. Play the odds -- look for hitters who walk frequently and don't strike out much, and only make exceptions for guys like Anderson and Guerrero who have a proven track record for defying the odds over several years.

Note: Ron Shandler and the staff at *The Forecaster* have done recent research on batting average that seems to be leading to more accurate batting average forecasts. Shandler believes that outside of a batter's ability to make contact, speed and power play the largest role in batting average. This likely explains why Alfonso Soriano manages to hit for a decent average every season despite an awful strikeout-to-walk ratio. This theory was first espoused in the 2003 edition of the *Forecaster,* and Shandler has provided more supporting evidence in the next two editions as well.

Ability to hit for power

Here are some good ways to evaluate a player's power-hitting ability:

1. *Home-run frequency.* Over the most recent seasons, is the player hitting more or fewer home runs per at-bat from year to year?

2. *Slugging percentage.* Young players who hit a lot of doubles but few home runs might be on the verge of becoming home run hitters.

3. *Does a player have power that doesn't manifest itself in his statistics?* Does he hit the ball hard or does he loop it over the infielder's heads? Does he make a lot of "noisy outs?" (Warning-track fly balls that are caught, line-drives caught by outfielders, etc.)

4. *Groundball / fly-ball ratio.* If you're going to get the ball out of the park, it must be in the air, so fly-ball hitters are logically better candidates to hit home runs.

By looking at these factors and examining the trends, you can get a better idea of future power production.

Base running ability

This is probably the hardest of the offensive skills to evaluate. A player's base running skills can affect not only how many bases he steals, but also how many runs he scores. Here are some things that may give you insight into a player's talents once he reaches base:

1. *Stolen-base attempts.* Does a manager allow a player to run much? Players who get the "green light" on the base paths are generally faster players.

2. *Stolen-base success frequency.* Unsuccessful base thieves often don't know how to read pitchers or don't pick up on pickoff moves easily, so their speed is negated. A player with a lot of attempts but a few steals could be a player who will steal more bases once he matures.

3. *Extra-base hits.* Players who are extremely fast often have high numbers of triples. On the contrary, don't count on steals from the home run hitter with relatively few doubles or triples among hits that don't leave the park.

4. *Base running smarts.* This is hard to gauge without watching a player for a long time. There are some guys without great speed who are good at reading pitchers and some who aren't that fast but steal bases on smarts.

Generally, the older a player gets, the fewer bases he'll steal, though there are exceptions like Otis Nixon who have career years in steals after their thirtieth birthday. Look at the trends in each of these areas and put them in context with a player's age.

One other point of note -- it's impossible to steal first, excepting what Lloyd McClendon did in 2003 during a fit of rage. (McClendon uprooted first base to protest an umpire's call.) Speed can only translate into stolen bases if a player reaches first base, and triple-A rosters are full of guys who can fly but can't stick at the major-league level because they can't get on base.

Talent-independent player factors

These are all player-specific factors, some of which the player has some control over (personality, conditioning, and work ethic) and some over which they player has no control (age, and, in some cases, health).

Age

Hitters' peak years are generally between 26 and 31. Some players produce terrific stats at age 23 or younger. If the player's stats look legitimate by the aforementioned standards, hold on to him because you may have a superstar in the making (Miguel Cabrera is an excellent current example). If a player is approaching or is in his mid-30's and seems to have hit a recent downward trend, watch out -- it could be the beginning of the end.

There are, of course, exceptions -- true superstars like Mark McGwire and Bonds, who had career years in their late thirties, or even Edgar Martinez, who had perhaps his best year ever at 40. In the past, the rule about a player's peak years was all but etched in stone, but lately, old age doesn't seem to be as big an obstacle as it was in the past. The increased pay for players no longer requires major leaguers to work a second job in the off-season to make ends meet as was the case decades ago; consequently, players have made conditioning a year-round effort. This has resulted in many veterans with the bodies of Olympic athletes well into their thirties. Advances in nutrition and sports medicine have also helped lengthen careers. (Many would argue that steroids have an impact too -- as this book was going to print, a slew of steroid scandals had just become public.) The coming decades may see a change in the thinking of baseball executives as age may come to mean less and less if thirty-something's continue having career years with greater regularity -- that is, provided those career years were attained by legitimate means.

Personality and work ethic

Some players have all the talent in the world but have it offset by a poor attitude and/or work ethic. Predicting performance for these players is difficult. Carl Everett, for example, seems to play like an all-star one year and self-destruct the next. Darryl Strawberry had a potential Hall-of-Fame career ruined by drug and behavioral problems. When projecting future performance for players who have unstable personalities (Milton

Bradley), it's usually best to forecast stats at a level that reflects something less than his optimal performance. This protects an owner against the disaster of paying top-dollar for a player who may self-destruct and get suspended or just have a poor year.

A player's mental state also bears watching for another reason. Most hitters go through at least two or three slumps of some degree during the year, and it's important that the player have enough confidence to snap out of it before it ruins his season. This is especially true of young players, who are often one prolonged slump away from a plane ticket to the minors. Occasionally, some players have distractions they can't seem to play through for an entire year, such as a divorce or a death in the family. If a player suddenly has a bad season and it can't be explained by an injury or a change in his surroundings, find out if he had off-field issues before forming an opinion about his future.

Conditioning and health

There are some players such as Ken Griffey, Jr. or Juan Gonzalez who just can't seem to stay healthy for more than a year or two at a time (In Griffey's case, staying healthy for two months is now an accomplishment). If a player has a long history of health problems, it's not wise to count on the player for a full year without at least one setback. On the other hand, the modern state of medicine is remarkable. Some injuries which once sidelined players for a year now keep players out only a few weeks, so some injuries are not as big a concern as they once were.

As I previously mentioned, players are taking advantage of new technologies, nutrition, workout supplements, and medicine to keep them in better shape than ever. This is usually a good thing, but not always. Be wary of players that look like defensive backs in October but resemble linebackers the next February -- the added muscle can sometimes rob them of flexibility and do more harm than good.

External factors

External factors have nothing to do with the player himself. These include:

The player's home park

Hitters generally put up better numbers in places like Colorado, Houston, and Milwaukee, and don't do as well in the pitcher-friendly environments of Los Angeles or Oakland.

Competition for playing time

Good players can get stuck on the bench or lose their jobs to minor-league phenoms who have just been promoted. I try to avoid players who may have regular jobs but don't have good skills and only put up numbers by virtue of playing time. These players usually don't keep jobs for long.

A player's manager and organization

There are certain managers and organizations that do things that have no good, logical explanation. Bob Boone (formerly of the Reds) and Pittsburgh's Lloyd McClendon seem to take joy in letting good players rot away on the bench while handing starting jobs to fringe players. (McClendon is especially stubborn; after three years of sitting Craig Wilson behind Larry, Curly, and Moe, Wilson finally cracked the lineup in 2004 after a torrid April made it obvious to even Loveable Lloyd that he deserved a full-time job. Even then, McClendon hit him sixth for several weeks.) Few things are more frustrating than owning a good player who sees three at-bats a week and plays behind a player with a .280 on-base percentage and no power.

Other players may not lose playing time but see their numbers suffer as a result of a manager's style, just as happened to Kenny Lofton in his brief time as a Brave. Lofton saw his steals decrease from 75 to 27 in his one year in Atlanta. Though Lofton was injured, much of this was due to manager Bobby Cox's managerial philosophy. Other organizations, such as Oakland and the new-look Red Sox, heavily favor station-to-station baseball at the expense of the stolen base.

His spot in the batting order

If the player is hitting between third and sixth in the batting order, RBI opportunities will be more abundant. If a player is hitting in one of the top two spots in the order, he's more likely to steal bases. If he's hitting seventh or eighth, he'll have fewer RBI opportunities and may be pitched around.

His teammates

Everything else being equal, a hitter is more likely to have a productive year if he's surrounded by good hitters.

Fielding ability

Technically this is more of a talent factor, but because it doesn't affect hitting ability, I've mentioned it here instead. Glove work is especially relevant in the NL because teams can't hide a weak fielder in the designated hitter's slot. Some players can hit but are such a disaster in the field that they're bound to lose playing time as a result. These are generally the very large power hitters, who occupy first base and left field, but the instance they quit hitting for power, their values as a players are gone and so are their jobs. And then there are players like Roger Cedeno, who runs like a deer but manages to play the outfield with the grace of a hippopotamus on ice skates.

Note: When choosing between a player who is mediocre but gets a lot of playing time and a player with good skills but lacking opportunity, I usually take the better player. Eventually most managers figure things out, but in extreme cases (Craig Wilson), that may take years. If not, there's always a chance the skilled benchwarmer could be traded to an organization that will use him. The A's, in particular, take full advantage of the ignorance of other organizations.

Evaluating pitchers

Pitchers can often be fairly evaluated just by looking at a few key stats. Here are the things size up when judging pitching talent:

Talent factors

The talent factors for pitchers include:

Control

You will generally not find a pitcher who averages more than four walks per nine innings on one of my fantasy rosters. Wild pitchers are bad for two reasons:

1. Poor control leads to walks and hit batsmen, which lead to more scoring chances for opponents, and;

2. Wildness is usually an indication that a player can't consistently throw to the area of the strike zone that he'd like, meaning he's prone to throwing pitches where hitters like to hit them.

Normally, I avoid wild pitchers. The only time I'll make an exception is if the pitcher also accumulates a large number of strikeouts. Some pitchers, like Roger Clemens and Nolan Ryan, were "effectively wild" at one point in their careers. Batters didn't get too comfortable against them because sometimes neither the pitcher nor the hitter knew whether the next pitch would wind up over the plate or under the hitter's chin. Obviously, this works to the pitcher's advantage.

The other exception would be the Tom Glavine-type of pitcher. Glavine, even at his peak, was never an overpowering pitcher like Clemens or Ryan; instead, he lives on the corners of the plate and relies on umpiring and undisciplined hitters for his success. Glavine has established that, even in his late-30's, he can consistently post mediocre strikeout-to-walk numbers and still succeed because he is the master of pitching around the hitters who can hurt him. Glavine will often walk the middle-of-the-order hitters to pitch to the lower-end batters. Watching Glavine pitch is something like watching Houdini try to wiggle out of a shark tank with rib eye steaks attached to each limb, but he's done it for so long with great success that it's just the norm for him. Poor Leo Mazzone must have kept Tums in business during Glavine's Atlanta career.

Strikeout ability

A top strikeout pitcher is someone who strikes out at least seven batters per nine innings and at least eight per nine if he's a reliever. Power pitchers are usually successful for these reasons:

1. *If a pitcher is striking hitters out regularly, it means that hitters generally find it hard to get a good read on a pitch, make effective contact and get on-base*, and;

2. *Fewer balls are put into play against the strikeout pitcher, meaning that batters have fewer chances to get hits.* Discount the hype about a pitcher's "stuff" unless he's got good strikeout numbers to match. This is especially true if the pitcher is a veteran who's never established any real success. Many owners draft pitchers based on a scouting report that talks about his pitch repertoire, his radar gun readings, or the comments made by some overzealous TV commentator. If the pitcher's repertoire is truly deceptive, he'll have the strikeout numbers to match the hype. While some pitchers are more talented than their numbers indicate, don't bother adding them to your roster until the numbers match the buzz.

Avoid pitchers who average less than one strikeout per two innings. If a pitcher cannot achieve at this level, he has little chance of long-term success. Also, be wary of pitchers with high strikeout numbers who give up unusually large amounts of hits on an annual basis. This probably means the pitcher is leaving way too many hittable pitches out over the heart of the plate. For years, Glendon Rusch had decent strikeout numbers but got hit hard anyway, though it appears he may have finally turned a corner in 2004.

Strikeouts-to-walks ratio

This is a great way to evaluate a pitcher because it's another measure of how well he locates pitches and how effective those pitches are. Look for pitchers who strike out twice as many batters as they walk.

Ability to prevent hits, especially extra-base hits

Does a pitcher give up a lot of homers or extra-base hits? Sometimes a pitcher can have good control, but because he's around the plate so much, he throws a lot of hittable pitches.

There are two things to consider. First, how often does the pitcher give up hits, and second, what kind of hits does he give up? Greg Maddux is not overpowering and may give up a lot of singles but rarely puts the ball where batters can tee off, so the hits result in minimal damage. Other pitchers like Curt Schilling or Bert Blyleven didn't give up a ton of hits but were notorious for giving up home runs. Since they gave up few hits overall, the homers often came with no one on base -- an indication that they are willing to take more risks in experimenting with a particular pitch or make a conscious decision to let the defense make the plays behind them rather than go for the strikeout. This is often the case when a pitcher has a big lead.

This is one of the hardest things about pitchers to predict, because hits allowed (other than home runs) are a product of several things. First, a team's ballpark can play a big part -- a place like Coors Field, where fielders have to play deep because of the altitude, or any place with artificial turf where grounders have a better chance of becoming singles than they would on grass. Second, the team's defense plays a big part -- if a pitcher has Ozzie Smith or Torii Hunter playing behind him, a batted ball that would go as a hit on most teams might turn into an out. Or, a team might be playing the infield in for a double-play ball, in which case something that would normally be an out can often scoot through the infield for a hit.

Note: There is a popular new theory proposed by baseball researcher Voros McCracken that says once a ball is put in play, luck primarily determines whether the ball becomes a hit or not unless that ball leaves the park. In other words, some pitchers get luckier than others if they have a good defense behind them (certainly true) but also some pitchers are lucky enough to have balls hit right at their fielders, while some are less fortunate and have the hits against them find holes in the defense. McCracken stumbled upon this theory while researching pitching performance from one year to the next. He found that across several seasons, the same pitcher could often display fairly-constant walk and strikeout numbers while his hit totals fluctuated extensively across the seasons.

While this is a relatively-new explanation, it's quickly become a generally-accepted conclusion within the baseball community. In fact, McCracken soon found a job with the Boston Red Sox because of these conclusions. There exists a certain group of pitchers that tend to buck McCracken's trends, but the stat heads are working to explain those pitchers as well.

Groundball and fly-ball tendencies

Publications like *The Forecaster* and *Sports Weekly* are starting to track pitcher tendencies from one year to the next. Obviously, you don't want to own a fly-ball pitcher in some place like Coors Field or The Metrodome, but it's not so bad in Oakland, Los Angeles, or San Francisco. And obviously, groundball pitchers should benefit more from a good infield behind them.

Talent-independent factors

As with hitters, pitchers have specific personality traits and mental make-ups that are mostly independent of God-given talent, but have plenty to do with their success. They are:

Poise and intelligence

Pardon the redundancy, but Glavine gives up larger numbers of base runners than you'd expect in a star pitcher, yet in his prime, he was always near the top of the ERA leader board every season. Pitchers with similar statistics can be explained by two things. First, they are smart. You rarely see these pitchers give great hitters good pitches. Glavine, in particular, will often go through the middle of a team's batting order and hardly throw a strike, but bear down against the seventh-through-ninth hitters because they're less likely to hurt him. Smart pitchers who have confidence in their stuff are often able to do this because they know their strengths and weaknesses as well as those of the hitters, so they simply pitch around guys until they find the right match-up -- even if it means loading the bases to get the situation they want.

Second, these pitchers don't get rattled in clutch situations such as when the bags are full. They're generally veterans who have been in those situations many times and they're usually less nervous than the hitters.

At one time, I looked at Glavine's raw numbers and felt his successful career was a fluke. However, I've learned that there's a reason for his success that goes beyond the obvious statistics.

Work ethic, conditioning, and injury history

Some pitchers like Clemens and Ryan were able to dominate into their forties because they were fanatics about conditioning (please don't ask me to explain David Wells). Then there are the Jeff D'Amico's of the world that are on the DL more than they are an active roster. Knowing a player's penchant for conditioning or if his past shows a tendency to be injury prone is very important when putting your roster together on draft day. Be especially cautious of young pitchers who throw a lot of innings before they turn 25 -- history shows they are good candidates for a major arm injury in their career at some point.

Age

Some pitchers are late bloomers, not achieving their greatest success until their late twenties or in their thirties. In 2002, for instance, perhaps the two best starting pitchers in baseball, Curt Schilling and Randy Johnson, were 35 and 39, respectively, and John Smoltz (arguably baseball's best closer that season) was 35. Clemens was pitching lights-out at 40, and Greg Maddux and Tom Glavine had All-Star years at 36. The first four guys on the list continued to throw as hard as most any pitcher in the game for the next couple of years, while the next two continued to get the job done more with guile than by blowing the ball by hitters.

What's the lesson here? Don't be scared to own older pitchers, especially if they are power pitchers. Some of them -- notably Johnson and Schilling -- struggled in their 20's but registered some of the best pitching seasons of the last two to three decades once they learned to pitch. Glavine and Maddux don't overpower hitters but have been remarkably effective. They know their limits and are good at outsmarting hitters, allowing them to see continued success after losing a couple miles per hour on their fastballs.

On the other hand, be more cautious with younger pitchers. Roy Oswalt, Barry Zito, Mark Mulder, and Kerry Wood had stellar years in their early-twenties, but more often you will see young pitchers struggle a bit before tasting success. Do not avoid young pitchers at all costs, but filling half a roster with promising pitchers without at least a year or two of sustained big-league success is not a formula for winning. Likewise, it is dangerous to write off a young pitcher with three or four rough years behind him if he showed irregular flashes of greatness. Sometimes a young pitcher just needs a couple months of success to gain the confidence that makes him successful.

I am not advocating building a fantasy staff with nothing but geezers, but given two pitchers of equal ability, one being younger than 25 and the other older than 30, I'd generally prefer the veteran.

External factors

Pitchers are probably more affected than hitters by external factors, which include:

The pitcher's home ballpark

You probably know which parks are hitters' parks, and those that are considered pitchers' parks. An extra note of caution here: avoid fly-ball pitchers in smaller parks or places with high altitude like Colorado.

His team's defense

Defense affects the number of hits allowed and runs scored; hence it affects ERA and Ratio (or WHIP) in Roto stats.

The pitcher's role

Some pitchers perform poorly as starters but succeed as relievers. Pay careful attention when a pitcher's role changes to see how he reacts. Sometimes, mediocre starters who only have one or two pitches they can throw for strikes will shine when handed the closer's role. Also, keep in mind that pitchers' ERA's often improve when they are sent to the bullpen for two reasons: one, they are used in situational roles (lefties facing left-handed hitters and righties facing right-handed hitters) which favor pitchers; and two, they often benefit by getting outs from the previous pitcher's base runners (as in the case of the reliever who induces a double play to the first hitter he faces and thus records two outs by facing one batter).

As a side note, history is full of pitchers who performed poorly as starters but excelled as relief aces. That role shift seems to work less-frequently in reverse.

Other pitchers in the organization or staff

Many less-than-stellar pitchers attain a closer's role by default because no one else in the organization was ready for it. Usually, these pitchers lose the job when the front office realizes they need a real closer and trade to get one.

His manager

Very often, young pitchers who deserve to be in a rotation find themselves sitting at AAA for a couple of years because certain organizations prefer veterans, no matter how bad they may be. Dusty Baker and some other managers are notorious for preferring veterans. Baker is the anti-Christ for young pitchers, because once he decides to use them, he fails to heed reasonable pitch-counts and inning limits. Not surprisingly, his pitchers sometimes get hurt before they reach the prime of their careers.

His pitching coach

Atlanta's Leo Mazzone and Cincinnati's Don Gullett are noted for getting good results from pitchers who are supposed to be "washed up." St. Louis's Dave Duncan is another good example -- witness what he did with Jason Marquis in 2004.

Note: When in doubt, draft a talented arm. I prefer quality pitchers who may not quite have a starter or closer's role nailed down over marginal ones who may have nailed down a #4 or #5 slot in his team's rotation or a player whose only redeeming quality is a good home park. A player with talent has a higher probability of success, but poor pitchers with good numbers by virtue of luck or factors beyond their control can quickly lose all value with a change in role or a trade. A quality pitcher can still help your team even if he's pitching in middle relief. If he's good enough, he may gain value if his manager promotes him to a larger role. As a general rule, lousy pitchers don't stay in starting or closing roles for long periods of time, and talented pitchers eventually land the plum roles.

Examining ERA's

I don't pay as much attention to a player's Earned Run Average when evaluating pitchers. There are a few reasons for this:

1. *One or two bad appearances can distort ERA for an entire season.* One terrible outing (for instance, an ill-fated trip to Coors Field) can add half a run or more to a pitcher's ERA for the year. Relievers are particularly affected by one bad outing due to the lower numbers of innings they throw.

2. *Pitchers are subject to things beyond their control.* If a pitcher leaves the game with the bases loaded, he can give up somewhere between zero and three more earned runs -- usually the difference between a successful or poor performance. A starting pitcher's ERA can vary considerably from year to year due to the quality of his relief.

3. *A pitcher's defense often determines whether a ball in play is a hit or an out.* This does not reflect the pitcher's true ability.

4. *ERA often is the product of other elements of good or bad luck.* Some days a pitcher may give up an inordinate amount of seeing-eye singles that are strung together to produce runs. Conversely, he may get hit hard on days when the wind keeps would-be homers in the park.

Over time, the law of averages takes over. Good pitchers should post good ERA's over time. If a good pitcher pitching in a good park has a bad ERA year, it's often a fluke. On the other hand, pitchers with average or poor walk and strikeout numbers may have a year or two with good ERA's, but these generally don't last long (though we noted the exceptions of wily veteran pitchers like Tom Glavine). Pay more attention to skill level and circumstances in predicting future ERA's than anything.

Making statistical projections

Now that we've thoroughly covered the nuts and bolts of player evaluation, it's time to briefly cover some ground rules of statistical projections. Here are some considerations to keep in mind as you predict each player's statistics for the following season:

1. History is your best guide. If a player has hit 25-30 home runs for each of the past five seasons, chances are that so long as everything else stays equal (health, ballpark, the lineup around him, etc.) he'll likely hit 25-30 home runs the next year.

2. Consider the direction a player's career is headed. If a player's career seems to be on a steady decline or up tick, you should probably keep your projections headed in that direction.

3. Consider all the outcomes. If a player is a potential 40-home run hitter when he's healthy for a full year but seems to miss 40 games every season (J.D. Drew, or worse, Ken Griffey, Jr.), take this into consideration and slot him for 30 homers instead of 40.

On the other hand, don't shortchange players with huge upsides just because they haven't produced the stats yet. A 27 year-old pitcher who's averaged ten wins the last three seasons but is showing skill improvement might win 18 the next season provided he's on a quality team. A 13 or 14-win projection might be more appropriate.

Be especially careful of players who begin the year on the DL, and really cautious of those coming off serious injuries. Players and managers alike can often be overly-optimistic in their prognosis for a quick recovery. I learned the hard way with Robb Nen in 2004. Needing a closer and finding few left on the draft board, I paid $18 for Nen, who I had projected for about 25 saves despite the fact that he'd missed the entire previous season with shoulder problems. He was supposed to return the second week of April, but instead, Nen never recovered and missed the entire season. In hindsight, I should have just taken my licks in saves and spent money towards building a surplus in other categories and trading for a closer later.

4. Be careful with rookies. A young pitcher may be the next Sandy Koufax, but don't expect 20 wins, 300 strikeouts, and a 2.50 ERA his first season. If you strongly believe he'll win 15 games with a 3.00 ERA, temper your expectations to about a dozen wins and perhaps a 3.50 ERA.

I once made this mistake with a young Paul Konerko, who looked like a legitimate candidate for 25 homers and a .300 batting average even as a rookie. Konerko turned out to be that good eventually, but he was slow out of the gate as a rookie and found himself in AAA. To make matters worse, the Dodgers gave up on him and eventually traded to Cincinnati, who collects corner outfielders and first basemen like Imelda Marcos collects shoes. He didn't play there either and got traded to the White Sox, who finally gave him a shot, but it was too late to do me any good.

A final note on talent, luck, and fluke seasons

If there's a "golden rule" of talent evaluation and player forecasts, it's this: play the percentages. Every season, several players have poor performances that are way out of context with their baseball career. They almost always return to their career norms the following seasons unless there is a valid explanation such as an injury or an extenuating personal circumstance.

On the other side of the coin, there will always be extreme career years. Brady Anderson hit 51 home runs at age 32 when his previous career high was 21. Chris Hammond posted a 0.95 ERA in 76 inning for the Braves in 2002 after being out of the majors for three years -- and out of baseball completely for two of those years. Neither player followed up with anything resembling those great campaigns the next year. Because one can rarely see these things coming, the smart play is to go with what you know and hope that the bad breaks are absorbed by an equal amount of unforeseeably-good events.

In other words, don't try to catch lightning in a bottle. Don't fret when Damian Moss, Elmer Dessens, and Tomo Ohka pitch out of their minds for a whole season and someone else wins the pennant (that happened to me in 2003). Even complete idiots hold the winning lotto ticket on occasion. Bet on the players with talent and a track record -- in the long-term, talent wins out over luck more often than not.

Moving forward

While these tips on how to project players are fresh on your mind, now is a good time to open a simple spreadsheet and project player statistics for the coming year. Save the spreadsheet (and save it often as you work on it) with these numbers as we will use it later in the book.

Third Inning

Standings points

Player value is one of the most widely-debated topics within fantasy baseball. Should an owner spend $30 on a slugger who hits 35 home runs or someone who steals 50 bases? Should he trade a player who registers 40 saves for a 20-game winner? Throw in the "average" categories like ERA, and batting average, and then mix hitters and pitchers together, and those questions become tougher to answer. Is the league's ERA leader worth more than the .330 hitter? Should you trade last year's batting champion for an ace closer?

In most leagues, value is often determined by a league consensus. If ten of a league's twelve owners will generally pay more for the power hitter than the closer, then it is assumed that the power hitter is more valuable. Large stat services, who keep track of hundreds of leagues across America, generally assume that data from a broad sample of leagues shed clues upon the correct answers. But does that make this true in either case?

"Ground rules" for standings points

To find the answers, we have to dig deeper. Here are some fundamental truths about standings points and how they contribute to player value:

1. Ultimately, an owner wins a league by accumulating more points in the standings than all other owners. Therefore, players who gain teams the most points in the standings are the most valuable players.

2. Individual players' standings points calculations serve as a common denominator to compare the slugger to the closer, and to put the ace starter on equal footing with the batting champion. For this reason, they serve as the backbone of the valuation system we'll create later in the book.

Those who have read books about fantasy value before are already familiar with the concept of standings points as a basis for player value. However, my opinions of standings points and their role in value vary somewhat from other writers. I'll add a few new wrinkles that should help owners build the best possible value systems for their leagues.

3. To create functional auction values, players should be evaluated from the perspective of the "average team." Problems in valuation arise because players have different value to different teams. To a team that needs 10 homers to gain four standings points, Barry Bonds has substantial value. But if Bonds is on the roster of a team 50 homers ahead of the second-place team, he's not-so valuable for that team.

Because of the variance from one team to the next, we'll use league standings reports to see how players would be valued on a typical team.

4. Standings point values differ across leagues. My twelve-team NL-only league may have a typical distance of five stolen bases between teams; yours may have eight. That means a 40-steal player would earn eight standings points in my league, but just five in yours. That's a substantial difference that shouldn't be ignored.

Why is this so? Every league's personality mix is different. One league might have a heavy bias towards power hitters and therefore the home run and RBI standings are probably very tight from one year to the next. Another may prefer relief aces to power hitters, so teams are closer together in saves and further apart in the hitting categories.

Many of the big stat services provide standings point differentials for use in calculating auction values. They average dozens, if not hundreds of leagues, in order to come up with standards to be used from one league to the next. As I've already demonstrated, this isn't the best way.

5. The past is the best predictor of the future. To find out how a league's owners might behave in the future, simply look to the league's standings history. Four or five years of year-end standings reports will likely provide a good idea of what those standings point differentials look like for a coming season.

Players in new leagues will take a different approach to the topic than those in established leagues. I'll start with instructions for existing leagues, but rookies should not skip that section in order to properly understand the latter section on new leagues.

Calculating standings points for established leagues

Players have positive or negative value in relation to how many points they gain or cost a fantasy team within a specific league. Because of this, we first need to know some information about the league in which we evaluate a player. The process begins with a look at each league's individual category standings.

Specifically, an owner needs to know what it generally takes to gain -- or lose -- points within a given league. Sometimes, a couple of pitching wins can move a team two or three points in the standings, but in other instances ten wins may gain the team nothing. Sometimes a hit or two can yield another batting average point, and other times, a .005 point bump in average is irrelevant. A home-run race could have five teams at the top separated by seven homers from top to bottom, but a 40-homer difference from sixth to seventh. The obstacles mount once multiple seasons are considered. One season, the top eight teams in stolen bases might be separated by 15 steals; the next, there might be 100 steals between the leader and the eighth-place finisher.

So, there are obvious problems in determining what constitutes value, since it varies from team to team and season to season. Solving the riddle is tough enough with these issues alone, and it is compounded further when looking to the future. After all, what we want to know is not so much whether 30 more runs batted in would have gained a team another standings point last year, but what those added RBI will do for you the next season.

Team total categories

There are two different kinds of categories for which we must calculate value: "Team average" categories such as batting average, WHIP, and ERA; and "team total" categories that deal in whole numbers such as home runs, RBI, saves, wins, etc. Each comes with its own set of issues; I will deal with team total categories for now and deal with the average calculations later.

Team total calculations are the easier of the two to handle. There are two tasks that are important -- finding the standings point differentials within each category (*i.e.,* what it takes to gain a standings point) and computing the number of standings points each player gains a team in each category.

Where to begin?

We already know that player value rises out of how much a player helps a team in the standings. Just as we get started, yet another question arises: Where does "value" begin? Consider this twelve team league's RBI standings:

Team	RBI	Standings Points
Team A	950	12
Team B	925	11
Team C	900	10
Team D	875	9
Team E	850	8
Team F	825	7
Team G	800	6
Team H	775	5
Team I	750	4
Team J	725	3
Team K	700	2
Team L	675	1

Right away, we know that 25 additional RBI gains each team a point until the team reaches the top of the standings, at which point additional RBI are of no help. The question becomes: "Do we consider the RBI it takes to start from last place as relevant?" In other words, do we focus on just the additional 25 RBI it takes to get from last to 11th-place, or should we concern ourselves with the other 775 RBI needed to get to 800?

After some experimentation with a "zero-based" system where I included those additional 775 RBI, I got some weird results -- some great hitters were worth 40% of a team's salary cap and some good hitters had little to no value. Of course, anyone who's played fantasy baseball knows that won't fly.

The reason this happens is because of the large variances within the raw numbers from one statistical category to the next. At the present time, Scott Podsednik or Juan Pierre can steal 60 or 70 bases in a single season. But in the twelve-team, NL-only league I play in, two teams didn't even reach 70 steals, and three more didn't break 100. If we included those 775 RBI in our total, the league's best hitters – who, at most, knock in 150 runs

-- wouldn't even account for 1/5 of a standings point. Meanwhile, the speed merchants of the world would demand all our money.

There are two other good reasons to start from last place:

1. In "team total" categories, most teams will accumulate some statistics whether they intend to do so or not. Even the worst fantasy team ever assembled will hit a few dozen homers and knock in a couple hundred runs or win 30-40 games. The usual exception to this is the saves category, and even there, a team can easily pick up a save or two by accident.

2. A value system should be based in reality. Since teams rarely accumulate zero stats in team-total categories (the "saves" category being a possible exception), why use an artificial condition as the basis of a value system?

Therefore, we'll start with the last place team in every category and work up the standings to determine our standings point differentials within each category.

Calculating league standings differentials in team total categories

To start, we need to know is how much of each unit it typically takes to gain a point in a certain category. Consider the home run standings for the past six years in my league, the Granny White Pikers' League (note: in 2000, we had only ten teams):

Granny White Piker's League- Home Runs

Totals	2002	2001	2000	1999	1998	1997
1st	267	321	350	358	338	266
2nd	259	262	345	275	238	196
3rd	235	247	342	270	232	189
4th	219	243	301	268	218	186
5th	212	235	260	233	214	185
6th	210	229	253	220	195	184
7th	208	228	246	202	179	159
8th	175	222	240	200	163	146
9th	173	219	211	180	158	134
10th	149	168	117	140	151	133
11th	148	167		138	143	121
12th	126	149		109	138	109

Differences	2002	2001	2000	1999	1998	1997	Average
1st to 2nd	8	59	5	83	100	70	
2nd to 3rd	24	15	3	5	6	7	
3rd to 4th	16	4	41	2	14	3	
4th to 5th	7	8	41	35	4	1	
5th to 6th	2	6	7	13	19	1	
6th to 7th	2	1	7	18	16	25	
7th to 8th	33	6	6	2	16	13	
8th to 9th	2	3	29	20	5	12	
9th to 10th	24	51	94	40	7	1	
10th to 11th	1	1		2	8	12	
11th to 12th	22	18		29	5	12	
Avg. Difference	12.82	15.64	25.89	22.64	18.18	14.27	*18.24*

Differences, in order	2002	2001	2000	1999	1998	1997	
	1	1		2	4	1	
	2	1	3	2	5	1	
	2	3	5	2	5	1	
	2	4	6	5	6	3	
	7	6	7	13	7	7	
Median	**8**	**6**	**7**	**18**	**8**	**12**	*9.83*
	16	8	29	20	14	12	
	22	15	41	29	16	12	
	24	18	41	35	16	13	
	24	51	94	40	19	25	
	33	59		83	100	70	

This provides some useful information, including:

1. How close the home run standings have been.   We can note the differences between teams in the home run category, and see how many home runs it generally takes to gain a point.

2. The trend of home runs in previous years. Is the distance between teams in homers getting greater or smaller, or not changing at all? In this case, it appears the category is becoming more competitive (*i.e.*, less distance between each team in homers).

From this chart, let's extract a couple of critical numbers:

1. Average six-year difference (18.24) -- this tells us, on average, how many home runs it takes to gain a standings point.

2. Average six-year median (9.83) -- the term "median" means the middle number of an ordered sequence. If there's an odd number of terms, that number is exactly in the middle (for instance, in a sequence of eleven numbers, the sixth number is the median). If there is an even number of terms, that number is the average of the middle two numbers (for instance if you have ten numbers, then average the fifth and sixth numbers of the sequence). This gauge paints an entirely different picture of the home run standings.

However, there are a few problems here as illustrated by the corresponding chart, specifically:

1. The teams who punted categories have skewed the standings. There were only one or two home runs separating teams in homers in many cases, especially near the top of the standings. But near the bottom, many teams quit playing and there were differences of 40 or more between teams. Using only the average, all those one or two home run differences are offset by the large gaps. Factoring in the median helps reflect the actual closeness at some points within the category.

2. In reality, the difference between the first and second-place teams is insignificant. Teams that won home runs often accumulated many more homers than they needed. In 2001 of our example, the team that won the league in homers won by 59, which was 58 more than the team needed.

The extra homers gained that team no additional points, so the extra homers are irrelevant to the standings.

3. 2000 was significantly different than the other years.   Our league temporarily contracted by two teams in 2002, and another team owner couldn't make the draft in person. Since that season, we've permanently gone back to twelve teams, so 2000 is an anomaly.

Back to the big picture: we've examined the past to predict the future. In this case, we want a good idea of how many home runs it would have typically taken for a team in this league to gain a standings point in homers in 2003. 2000 would not have been a good predictor for 2003 for reasons I mentioned above. Also notice that the difference between the average and the median here is significant, and instinctively this should tell us a couple of things:

1. The average and the median are so far apart that it would probably be foolish to choose only one of the two (we'll consider this in a moment), and;

2. The irrelevant homers present a problem. One simple solution is to eliminate the needless home runs that the first-place teams accumulate. In other words, if a team wins homers by 59, count it as if they only won by one. Once the "59" becomes a "one," the critical numbers change. We'll call these new numbers the "relevant average" and "relevant median." Now, here's a new chart:

Granny White Piker's League- Home Runs

Differences, in order	2002	2001	2000	1999	1998	1997	*Average*	W/O 2000
	1	1		2	4	1		
	2	1	3	2	5	1		
	2	3	5	2	5	1		
	2	4	6	5	6	3		
	7	6	7	13	7	7		
Median	8	6	7	18	8	12	9.83	9.31
	16	8	29	20	14	12		
	22	15	41	29	16	12		
	24	18	41	35	16	13		
	24	51	94	40	19	25		
	33	59		83	100	70		
Avg. Difference	12.82	15.64	25.89	22.64	18.18	14.27	18.24	16.71

Adjusted differences, in order	2002	2001	2000	1999	1998	1997	*Average*	W/O 2000
	1	1		*1*	1	1		
	1	1	*1*	2	4	1		
	2	1	*3*	2	5	1		
	2	3	*6*	2	5	1		
	2	4	*7*	5	6	3		
Average Relevant Median	7	6	7	*13*	7	7	7.83	8.00
	16	6	*29*	*18*	8	12		
	22	8	*41*	*20*	14	12		
	24	15	*41*	*29*	16	12		
	24	18	94	*35*	16	13		
	33	51		40	19	25		
Average Relevant Difference	12.18	10.36	20.82	15.18	9.18	8.00	12.62	10.98

This makes a major difference. Including 2000, the relevant median is now 7.83 and the average difference between teams in home runs has shrunk to 12.62 -- differences of two and 5.62 respectively from the old numbers. Throwing out 2000, the median becomes eight and the relevant difference 10.98.

So what does one do with all these numbers? With the adjustments for relevancy, the median and differences become significantly closer, especially with 2000 discarded. The reason for the difference, of course, is the teams towards the bottom of the standings who gave up in homers. Herein lies the problem -- both numbers are somewhat descriptive of what is happening, so which one should be used?

In my opinion, the solution is to average the relevant median and the relevant average over a period of several years. In this example, the numbers (throwing out 2000) would be 10.98 and 8, the average of which is 9.49. This should be a good home run standings point estimate for the GWPL in 2003. It acknowledges the effects of the poor teams within each category while considering them with the league's overall competitive balance.

In summary, here are my suggestions for calculating standings points:

1. Ignore the un-adjusted averages and medians, for reasons just discussed.

2. Throw out misleading data. If past seasons don't fall in line with the current patterns of your league, cast them aside.

3. Calculate the relevant averages and relevant medians over a several-year period and average those numbers.

4. Make adjustments if historical data doesn't reflect the changing face of a league. If any of the following scenarios are happening, you may need to tweak future standings point estimates:

A. Is a commodity becoming scarcer, more abundant, or staying the same? If home runs become scarcer for two or more straight seasons, it may be appropriate to decrease the home run standings-point differentials. I would not recommend making adjustments based on one season unless there is a change that's too large to ignore, such as a 10% change or more across the board in a particular statistical category.

B. Is a league becoming more or less competitive? If a league finally dumps those two owners who stop paying attention in mid-May every season and replaces them with better candidates, each category's standings will probably become more closely-contested. An owner should probably adjust standings points numbers accordingly.

C. Are there changes in the way a league values categories? Generally speaking, leagues may intentionally or unintentionally place more value on one category than another. (You'll see how this works later.) For instance, if a couple of owners decide not to buy any closers, this makes the differences between teams in saves larger than if all teams in the league bought closers. Note any trends in owner or league behavior within categories and make the corresponding adjustments if needed.

If the answer to all these questions is "no," stick with the average of the relevant averages and medians.

Calculating standings points for players in team total categories

Suppose that Sammy Sosa is expected to hit 52 homers in 2005. The calculation for Sosa's contribution in the home run standings is simple:

Sosa's home runs / League's standings point differential

$$52 / 9.49 = 5.48$$

Sosa gains a team about 5.48 places in home runs.

Team average categories

As with team total categories, league standings-point differentials must be calculated and then individual players' contributions tallied accordingly. But this time, there's an in-between step of calculating team benchmarks; I'll explain the relevance of that step in a moment.

Calculating league standings differentials in team average categories

Figuring standings point differentials for team average categories is similar to the process for "team total" categories. Consider the GWPL standings in recent years:

Chris Lee

Granny White Piker's League- Earned Run Average

Totals	2002	2001	2000	1999	1998	1997	*Average*	W/O 2000
1st	3.43	3.762	3.968	3.58	3.675	3.41		
2nd	3.521	3.771	4.188	4.02	3.79	3.61		
3rd	3.652	3.886	4.309	4.037	3.864	3.77		
4th	3.683	3.887	4.387	4.13	4.019	3.79		
5th	3.765	4.194	4.427	4.412	4.044	4.11		
6th	3.771	4.27	4.455	4.551	4.067	4.12		
7th	4.016	4.278	4.458	4.62	4.136	4.14		
8th	4.208	4.473	4.554	4.7	4.401	4.22		
9th	4.219	4.519	4.591	4.773	4.425	4.38		
10th	4.284	4.597	4.839	4.876	4.478	4.42		
11th	4.377	4.76		5.031	4.524	4.58		
12th	4.392	4.844		5.112	4.675	4.71		
Average ERA	*3.943*	*4.270*	*4.418*	*4.487*	*4.175*	*4.105*	*4.233*	*4.196*
Median ERA	**3.894**	**4.274**	**4.457**	**4.586**	**4.102**	**4.130**	**4.240**	**4.197**
Differences, in order	0.006	0.001		0.017	0.023	0.01		
	0.011	0.008	0.003	0.069	0.024	**0.02**		
	0.015	0.009	0.028	0.073	0.025	0.02		
	0.031	0.046	0.037	0.08	0.046	0.04		
	0.065	0.076	0.04	0.081	0.053	0.08		
Median	**0.082**	**0.078**	**0.078**	**0.093**	**0.069**	**0.13**	*0.088*	*0.090*
	0.091	0.084	0.096	0.103	0.074	0.16		
	0.093	0.115	0.121	0.139	0.115	0.16		
	0.131	0.163	0.22	0.155	0.151	0.16		
	0.192	0.195	0.248	0.282	0.155	0.2		
	0.245	0.307		0.44	0.265	0.32		
Avg. Difference	**0.087**	**0.098**	**0.097**	**0.139**	**0.091**	**0.118**	*0.105*	*0.107*
Relevant differences	0.001	0.001		0.001	0.001	0.001		
	0.006	0.001	0.001	0.017	0.023	0.01		
	0.011	0.008	0.003	0.069	0.024	0.02		
	0.015	0.046	0.028	0.073	0.025	0.02		
	0.031	0.076	0.037	0.08	0.046	0.04		
	0.065	**0.078**	**0.04**	**0.081**	**0.053**	**0.08**	*0.066*	*0.071*
	0.082	0.084	0.078	0.093	0.069	0.13		
	0.093	0.115	0.096	0.103	0.074	0.16		
	0.131	0.163	0.121	0.139	0.151	0.16		
	0.192	0.195	0.248	0.155	0.155	0.16		
Relevant differences,	0.245	0.307		0.282	0.265	0.32		
in order	**0.079**	**0.098**	**0.072**	**0.099**	**0.081**	**0.100**	*0.088*	*0.091*

As is the case with team total categories, finding the standings point differential is an easy exercise once you weed out some of the data. As was the case with homers, there's a difference between the relevant and un-adjusted numbers. Throwing out 2000, the relevant medians and differences are .071 and .091 -- an average of .081. However, the calculations get tougher when we estimate a single player's impact within an "average" category. First, we must find a starting point for determining

54

whether a player helps or hurts teams in average categories. We'll call this a "team average benchmark."

Calculating team average benchmarks

There is a debate among valuation experts as to how the previously-mentioned matter of "impact" should be measured. With team total categories, we started from the last-place team and moved up. Some believe team average categories should be approached in the same way. I disagree for reasons outlined earlier -- players should be measured by their impact on the average team. By starting from the bottom, any pitcher with an ERA below 4.71, 4.68, 5.11, 4.84, 4.84, and 4.39 respectively between 1997 and 2002 would theoretically help a team's ERA. But if you were a GWPL owner in 2002, when the average team ERA was 3.94 and the median ERA was 3.89, would you draft all the 4.38 ERA pitchers you could to "help" your ERA? Of course not.

The other implicit question is whether the average ERA should be the average of the pitchers in the draft pool or of the expected team average at the year's end. First of all, using the draft pool average would be circular and therefore impossible. The draft pool average cannot be computed without first defining the draft pool, which requires owners to first define that point which players help or hurt a team. Second, there is the matter of relevancy. As previously mentioned, the basis for true player value is found by measuring how much the player helps or hurts a team over the entire season. Free agent acquisitions are inevitable in virtually every league, and free agent pitchers as a whole are always worse than drafted pitchers. The same goes for hitters and batting average. Failure to account for this would just be foolish.

Calculating standings points for individual players in team average categories

Determining each player's impact in team average categories is more difficult than the same exercise in team total statistics. I'll use ERA as an example and walk through the steps in the process:

1. Calculate the critical component numbers for each player. In this case, we need the evaluated player's innings pitched and earned runs allowed. (We'll call him "Player X.") Let's take Greg Maddux as an example, and suppose that we expect him to pitch 200 innings in 2003 with a 3.15 ERA, which means he allows 70 earned runs.

2. Calculate the component numbers for the average team. Here, we need the innings pitched and earned runs for the league's average team. Let's suppose that the average GWPL team, which has ten pitchers, will throw 1,170 innings and allow 527 runs for a 4.054 ERA. (That's as close as I could get to 4.058 without using a fraction for the team's earned runs number.)

3. Calculate the component numbers for the base team. One thing to remember here is that Maddux's inclusion on the staff means the exclusion of another pitcher, whom we'll call Average Pitcher Y. Average Pitcher Y pitches 117 innings and allows 52.7 runs -- exactly 1/10 of the average team's total. The average staff without Average Pitcher Y now pitches 1,053 innings and allows 474.3 earned runs; we'll refer to this as the "base team" because it will serve as the foundation to measure each individual player's addition to a typical roster.

4. Calculate the base team's new critical numbers with the evaluated player. If we add Maddux to this staff, the team's numbers become 1,253 innings (1053 + 200) and 544.3 earned runs (474.3 + 70).

5. Calculate the base team's average with the evaluated player. The algebraic equation for ERA is:

$$(\text{Earned runs} / \text{innings pitched}) \times 9$$

With Maddux, the new ERA is (544.3 / 1,253) x 9 = 3.9095, which we'll round to 3.910.

6. Measure the evaluated player's impact. The old ERA was 4.054, the new is 3.910. Maddux should improve the average team's ERA by 0.144 runs.

7. Convert the evaluated player's impact to standings points. Earlier, I decided to use .081 as my ERA standings point differential. Dividing Maddux's impact by the ERA differential and rounding to two decimal places, we get:

$$(0.144 / .081) = 1.78$$

Maddux should help the average team by 1.78 places in the ERA standings.

As you've probably guessed by now, players can hurt teams in team average categories. This is not the case in team total categories, where although players can fail to *help* you much at times, they can't actually cause you to *lose* points as they do in team average standings.

For example, let's take Mike Hampton, who we expect to log 200 innings of a 5.00 ERA for 2003, which means he'll allow 111 earned runs. Here's how Hampton affects an average team's ERA:

Add Hampton to the base team and calculate the team's new ERA:
$$((474.3 + 111) / (1,054 + 200)) \times 9$$
$$(585.3 \ / 1,254) \times 9$$
$$4.199$$

Hampton's ERA impact is:
$$4.054 - 4.199 = -0.145$$
ERA rises by 0.145

Hampton's standings-point impact:
$$-0.145 / .081 = -1.79$$
Hampton costs his team 1.79 points in ERA

Mike Hampton would hurt the average team by 1.79 places in the standings, coincidentally, almost the same amount as his (then) Braves' teammate Maddux would help the average team.

Calculating a player's impact in team average categories isn't easy at first, but once you do it a few times it becomes fairly simple. In case you get lost, here are some simple steps to remember any time you need to calculate standings points in team average categories:

1. Calculate the league benchmark (league average) and critical numbers (innings pitched, earned runs, at-bats, hits, etc.).

2. Calculate the critical numbers for the base team (the average team less one average player).

3. Add the statistics of the player to be evaluated.

4. Find the new team average with that player.

5. Calculate his standings point impact.

6. Divide that number by the category's standings point differential.

Relative Category Value

Before we wrap up our discussion of standings points, there's one other topic that merits discussion, and that is how to value categories relative to each other.

Many of the valuation experts build their systems on these two principles:

1. The sum of standings points in team average categories for all players in the draft pool is zero. In other words, for every point gained by players in team average categories, the gain is offset by an equal point loss, making the sum of all points zero. As I've already stated, I disagree because this method doesn't include the potential impact of free agents. It also forces you to perform some very painful mathematical gymnastics to set the total league standings points in team average categories to zero, as you'll see later.

2. All team total categories are always assigned equal weight. The prevailing thought in most fantasy circles is that if there are 250 standings-gain points for the draft pool in homers, there must be 250 standings-gain points in stolen bases as well. This forces you to manipulate the standings numbers in order to generate the desired outcome of equalizing the categories. This is probably the proper approach for new leagues because there is no data to go on, but for existing leagues, I disagree. To illustrate why, consider this hypothetical league which uses only two categories -- steals and homers:

Homers		*#*	*St. Pts.*	*Steals*		*#*	*St. Pts.*
Team	A	325	10	Team J		145	10
Team	B	300	9	Team H		144	9
Team	C	275	8	Team B		143	8
Team	D	250	7	Team D		142	7
Team	E	225	6	Team A		141	6
Team	F	200	5	Team I		140	5
Team	G	175	4	Team J		139	4
Team	H	150	3	Team C		138	3
Team	I	125	2	Team E		137	2
Team	J	100	1	Team F		136	1

There are 2,125 total homers in this league, and 1,405 total steals. Generally speaking, there are 25 homers separating each team but only one steal between each. (For simplicity's sake, forget about the relevancy adjustment for now.) If we want to find the total standings points by category, we divide the homers and the steals by their standings point differences as follows:

Total standings points for homers:
2,125 / 25 = 85

Total standings points for steals:
1,405 / 1 = 1,405

Under the prevailing wisdom, we have to adjust the standings point differentials until the total numbers of standings points are equal for both categories. In other words, we need to generate an outcome whereby there are either 85 total standings points gained by all players in the league in both steals and homers, 1,405 standings points within the player pool for both steals and homers, or some in-between number where the figures are equal. Let's try making both categories have 1,405 standings points by dividing the steals standings points by the homers standings points:

Divide total steals by total homers:
1,405 / 85 = 16.53

What this means that in order to make home run standings points have a value equivalent to steals, we have to pretend that teams are generally separated by 16.53 steals instead of one. So, we've engineered our desired outcome, but does this seem right? If you could choose between a player who hit 25 homers or stole 17 bases, which would *you* pick?

The problem with "equal weighting" is that it doesn't value players according to their true worth. Though I've purposely used an extreme example, it demonstrates why you shouldn't manipulate standings point numbers so they jive with conventional wisdom.

The truth is that the personalities of your league influence your value system, and you'd better account for it if you want to win. If a league has power-hungry owners, the standings in homers and RBI are probably going to be closer. This lowers the home run and RBI differentials and generates more standings points within those categories. In the end, rigging the numbers will generate an inaccurate set of dollar values for your league. Let the numbers speak for themselves.

Standings points for new leagues

It may be difficult to calculate standings points for new leagues because there is no history. There are two possible ways to solve the problem:

1. Find data from another similar league or leagues. First, try to find an existing league with similar categories and number of owners. Examine their stats and make the calculations just as I demonstrated in the previous pages. The more leagues you can find, the better. Occasionally, stat services make these numbers public; you might try *USA Stats* (usastats. com), though I don't think they've done this in recent years.

2. Attempt to weight all categories equally. While I don't like this for existing leagues, new leagues have no history and therefore no demonstrated biases. The safe bet is to assume no bias and count all categories the same.

The difficulty will come in setting benchmarks for average categories, but major league averages might be of help. Remember though, that your league's averages will be different than the AL or NL average. If the American League hits .260 as a whole, an owner would likely choose a figure closer to .265 or perhaps higher because many of the lower-end hitters won't be worth roster spots on a fantasy team. In the NL, the proper figure might be closer to .270 because the NL average includes batting stats of pitchers, which do not come into play in fantasy ball.

Creating a spreadsheet

There is no better way to keep track of player projections and to later figure player value than to use a spreadsheet. If you have access to a computer, go ahead and open a blank spreadsheet now, as I will demonstrate how to put projections into a spreadsheet and later use that sheet to value players. There will be several phases across several chapters, and the first phase begins now.

My spreadsheet example will be geared around traditional, "4x4" leagues that use the original eight Rotisserie ™ categories -- home runs, RBI, stolen bases, and batting average for offense, and wins, saves, earned run average, and "ratio" (or "WHIP," if you prefer). In my example, I will put both hitters and pitchers on the same sheet, and a strongly urge you to do the same. I will be using actual statistics from the 2002 season as my "projected" numbers.

Final notes before we begin: Explaining how to build a spreadsheet is an arduous task, especially if the audience includes some who have never used one. I've kept things as simple as possible and frequently include illustrations of a sample sheet. If you get lost, flip ahead and back to the included examples and that should help you find your way. Also, be sure and save a copy of what you're doing every few minutes. The last thing you need is for a computer crash or power outage to undo your hard work.

Spreadsheet phase one: Enter player forecasts for the first hitter and pitcher

"Phase one" of building a spreadsheet consists of entering player forecasts for one hitter and one pitcher who is eligible in your league.

1. Going across your sheet, enter column headings for hitters, including statistical categories and player positions. I have started with the hitters and have created a positional grid for every non-pitching position and will use the 2001 stats for Mark Grace and Curt Schilling as my examples. Once you have run out of positions, enter "PO" to signify "position." You will need this cell later to sort players by position.

Then, enter column headings for all needed hitting statistics. I have entered one hitter and suggest you do the same to get a feel for what you'll be doing.

To do this in the most efficient manner, set your sheet up exactly as I do mine. If your league uses different categories, set yours up as closely to mine as you can. That way, you can follow along with my examples and charts if you become confused. Your chart will look something like this:

	A	B	C	D	E	F	G	H	I	J	K	L	M	N
1	Hitter	C	1	2	3	S	O	PO	AB	H	HR	RBI	SB	AVG
2	Grace, Mark								298	75	7	48	2	252

Note the entry in the batting average column. Instead of just entering a batter's projected average, let the spreadsheet make the calculation for you. Here's how batting average is calculated:

Batting average:

Hits / At-bats

Chris Lee

Grace's batting average calculation in cell n2:
= (j2/i2)*1000

Please note: The actual calculation for batting average is =(j2/i2).
I added the "*1000*" so that Grace's batting average would appear as a
whole number and not as a decimal with a preceding "zero."

*2. Repeat step one for the pitcher, making sure you line up the column
headers properly with the hitting statistics.*

My chart, with just one hitter and pitcher, looks like this:

	A	B	C	D	E	F	G	H	I	J	K	L	M	N	O	P
1	Hitter	C	1	2	3	S	O	PO	AB	H	HR	RBI	SB	AVG		
2	Grace, Mark								298	75	7	48	2	252		
3	Pitcher								W	SV	IP	H	ER	BB	ERA	RAT
4	Schilling, Curt								23	0	259	216	93	33	3.23	0.96

As with Grace's batting average, I have made the calculations for
Schilling's ratio and ERA. They are:

Earned run average:

(Earned runs / Innings pitched) x 9

Schilling's ERA calculation in cell 04:
(Cell m4 / cell k4) x 9
=(m4/k4)*9

Ratio (or, "WHIP"):

(Hits + walks) / Innings pitched

Schilling's ratio calculation in cell p4:
(Cell L4 + cell n4) / cell k4
=(L4+n4)/k4

Spreadsheet note: I have done several things with my sheet to make
viewing it easier. First, I have centered most of my cells on the sheet, put
column headings in bold, set most of the cells to "auto fit" or "best fit" to
eliminate wasted column space, and set most of the decimals to two points.

All these may be done through the "format" menu at the top of the sheet; see the spreadsheet's "help" menu if you can't figure it out on your own.

Spreadsheet phase two: Standings point phase

Open another spreadsheet, and set up the column headers to contain all key statistics in the same order as the sheet you've already created. Enter the statistics of the first hitter and first pitcher listed. We will begin to calculate their standings point values.

1. On the hitting and pitching header rows, enter column headings for calculating standings points. For hitters, I've entered the following after leaving two empty columns following the "AVG" row (this makes the hitting standings point columns line up with the pitching columns, as you'll soon see):

- "HP" for "home run points"
- "RP" for "RBI points"
- "SP" for "stolen base points"
- "AP" for "batting average points"

For pitchers, start the column headings immediately after the "RAT" header:

- "WP" for "win points"
- "SP" for "save points,"
- "EP" for "ERA points"
- "RP" for "ratio points"

Notice in the following example how the hitting and pitching standings point columns are lined up with each other.

2. Enter a blank row above the hitting row header. Repeat this for the pitching row header.

3. In the newly-created blank hitting row, enter "Standings differentials," in the hitters' column, and enter your standings-point differentials for each category in the corresponding standings point category. Do the same for pitchers.

4. Enter formulas to calculate standings points for players in team total categories. Here are the examples of how I computed those numbers for each of the five team total categories, using Mark Grace and Curt Schilling as examples. I have included the numerical calculations from my sheet in parentheses and italics so the examples are easier to follow.

Hitters

Home run standings points:

Grace's home run standings point cell:
Grace's home runs / League home run differential
(7 / 8.5)

Formula for my sheet in cell q3:
= Cell k2 / absolute cell q1
=k3/q1

Spreadsheet note: This is the first case in which we'll use something called an *absolute cell reference.* Absolute cell references are used to designate that a particular cell's contents remain constant once the "copy" function is used. In our case, we will later copy standings point formulas to other cells so that they will read the home run numbers for all the particular players, but we always want the sheet to read the home run differential contained in cell q1. Hence, we use an absolute reference that always points back to that particular cell.

The formula for absolute references is always as follows: **$column letter$row number**

RBI standings points:

Grace's RBI standings point cell:
Grace's RBI / League RBI differential
(48 / 21)

Formula for my sheet in cell r3:
= Cell L3 / absolute cell r1
=L3/r1

Stolen base points:

Grace's stolen base standings point cell:
Grace's stolen bases / league stolen base differential
(2 / 5.5)

Formula for my sheet's cell s3:
= Cell m3 / absolute cell s1
=m3/s1

Pitchers

Wins standings points:

Schilling's win standings point cell:
Schilling's wins / league win differential
(23 /3.5)

In my cell q6:
= Cell i6 /absolute cell q4
=i6/q4

Saves standings points:

Schilling's saves standings point cell:
Schilling's saves / league saves differential
(0 / 5)

My sheet's cell r6:
= Cell j6 / absolute cell r4
=j6/r4

Your sheet should now look like this:

	A	Q	R	S	T
1	Standings differentials	8.5	21	5.5	0.002
2	**Hitter**	**HP**	**RP**	**SP**	**AP**
3	Grace, Mark	0.8	2.3	0.4	
4	Standings differentials	3.5	5	0.075	0.018
5	**Pitcher**	**WP**	**SP**	**EP**	**RP**
6	Schilling, Curt	6.6	0		

5. Enter three blank rows above both the hitting "standings differentials" row and four blank lines before the pitching "standings differentials" row. These rows will be used to make team average standings point calculations. The extra row before the pitching section is simply to divide the hitting and pitching portions of the sheet.

6. Enter row header labels in the newly-created rows. Use the following labels for hitters:

- "Number of hitters:"
- "Benchmark hitter"
- "Base team"

For pitchers:

- "Number of pitchers:"
- "Benchmark pitcher"
- "Base team"

Leave the row before "benchmark pitcher" blank to separate hitters from pitchers.

7. Enter the number of hitters and pitchers allowed per team in the cell just to the right of the "number of hitters" and "number of pitchers" entries. These numbers should be entered in cells b1 and b8 if you are following my example.

8. Enter benchmark player stats to be used to calculate standings points in team total categories. You may have already calculated these in Inning Two; **if you have**, enter these numbers in the corresponding cells above the proper row header. (For instance, if your benchmark batting average is .271 as mine is, enter this in the batting average column in the benchmark player's row.) In mine, I'll enter at-bats in i2 and hits in j2. Also, enter the hits and at-bats of your league's benchmark hitter. Repeat the same process, including the critical numbers (innings pitched, earned runs, hits, and walks) for pitchers. Then, skip to step nine.

If you haven't already calculated these numbers, do this now. Refer to the section entitled "Calculating standings points in team average categories" earlier in this chapter.

You do not need to calculate benchmark stats for any team total categories.

9. Enter base team totals. "Base teams," as you probably remember, consist of the average team minus one average player. They will be used to calculate typical player impact in team average categories. Copy these results to the corresponding "base team" cells.

Spreadsheet note: In most spreadsheets, the mathematical symbol for multiplication is the "*" symbol, which is normally found on the "8" key on your keyboard.

Here's how I'll calculate all my base team numbers. The actual numbers in my example are included in parentheses.

Hitters

At-bats, base team:

At-bats of benchmark hitter x (# of hitters per team minus one)
(450 x (14 - 1))

Formula for my sheet in cell i3:
= at-bats cell of benchmark hitter x # of hitters cell
=i2*(b1-1)

Hits, base team:

Hits of benchmark hitter x (# of hitters per team minus one)
(122 x (14 - 1))

Formula for my sheet in cell j3:
= hits of benchmark hitter cell x (# of hitters cell – 1)
=j2*(b1-1)

Pitchers

Innings pitched, base team:

Innings pitched of benchmark pitcher x (# of pitchers per team minus one)

Formula for my sheet in k10:
= innings pitched of benchmark pitcher cell x (# of pitchers cell – 1)
=k9*(b8-1)

Hits allowed, base team:

Hits allowed by benchmark pitcher x (# of pitchers per team minus one)

Formula for my sheet in L10:
= hits of benchmark pitcher cell x (# of pitchers cell – 1)
=L9*(b8-1)

Earned runs allowed, base team:

Earned runs allowed of benchmark pitcher x (# of pitchers per team minus one)

Formula for my sheet in m10:
= earned runs of benchmark pitcher cell x (# of pitchers cell – 1)
=m9*(b8-1)

Walks allowed, base team:

Walks allowed by benchmark pitcher x (# of pitchers per team minus one)

Formula for my sheet n10:
= walks allowed of benchmark pitcher cell x (# of pitchers cell – 1)
=n9*(b8-1)

You'll also want to enter and compute the base team average figures if you haven't already, and enter them on your sheet as I have done. Your sheet should now look something like this (again, please note that I'm only showing one hitter and one pitcher for simplicity's sake):

	A	B	I	J	K	L	M	N	O	P	Q	R	S	T
1	Number of hitters:	14												
2	Benchmark hitter		450	122				0.2711						
3	Base team		5850	1586				0.2711						
4	Standings differentials										8.5	21	5.5	0.002
5	**Hitter**	**C**	**AB**	**H**	**HR**	**RBI**	**SB**	**AVG**			**HP**	**RP**	**SP**	**AP**
6	Grace, Mark		298	75	7	48	2	252			0.8	2.3	0.4	
7														
8	Number of pitchers:	9												
9	Benchmark pitcher				135	135	63	45	4.20	1.33				
10	Base team				1080	1080	504	360	4.20	1.33				
11	Standings differentials										3.5	5	0.075	0.018
12	**Pitcher**		**W**	**SV**	**IP**	**H**	**ER**	**BB**	**ERA**	**RAT**	**WP**	**SP**	**EP**	**RP**
13	Schilling, Curt		23	0	259.33	216	93	33	3.23	0.96	6.6	0		

10. Enter formulas to calculate all standings point numbers for team average categories for the first hitter and pitcher listed. This is the most complicated part of the spreadsheet because we have to measure each pitcher's impact upon the base team. We must calculate new stats for the team with each pitcher and hitter, measure that pitcher's impact on team average categories, and convert that to standings points. I will sometimes refer to the examined player as "Player X." First, I'll walk you through the reasoning and algebra of the formulas, and then I'll show you how to convert those formulas to spreadsheet formulas.

Hitters

Batting average with Player X:

Grace's stats: 298 AB, 75 H
Base team: 5,850 AB, 1,586 H

Add Grace to base team:
6,148 AB (5,850 + 298)
1,661 H (75 + 1,586)

Calculate base team's average with Grace:
1661 / 6148 = .2702

Grace's impact on batting average:
Base team average - base team average with Grace
.2711 - .2702 = .0009

Grace decreases a team's batting average by .0009

Each .002 gain in batting average is worth a standings point; conversely, each time a hitter costs his team .002 in batting average, it's worth a negative standings point. Here's how we measure Grace's standings point impact in batting average:

Batting average standings points of Player X:

Grace's batting average impact / league batting avg. differential:
-.0009 / .0020 = -0.45
(My numbers again differ from the example due to rounding)

Now, let's condense this to a formula:

= ((Player X's H + Base team's H) /
(Player X's AB + Base team's AB) - Base team batting average) /
league batting average differential

If you're using the same cells I'm using, the formula is as follows:

Formula for my cell t6:
= ((Grace hits cell + base team hits cell) /
(Grace at-bats cell + base team at-bats cell) – base team batting average cell)/
league batting average differential cell
=((j6+j3)/(i6+i3)-n3)/t4

Note: Be sure to use absolute cell references when referring back to base team totals and base team averages. Also, be careful to use the exact number of parentheses required; otherwise, your formula could be wrong.

Pitchers

Here's how I made the two calculations involving Schilling:

Earned run average with Player X:

Schilling's stats: 259.33 IP, 93 ER
Base team: 1,080 IP, 504 ER

Add Schilling to base team:
1,339.33 IP (259.33 + 1,080)
597 ER (93 + 504)

Calculate base team ERA with Schilling:
(597 / 1,339.33) x 9 = 4.012

Measure Schilling's impact on base team ERA:
Base team ERA before Schilling - ERA with Schilling
4.20 - 4.012 = 0.188

Schilling decreases team's ERA by .188

In this league, a pitcher gains a team a standings point in ERA for every .075 by which he lowers the team's ERA. To measure Schilling's ERA impact, we divide the ERA decrease caused by Schilling by the ERA standings point differential:

ERA standings impact of Player X:

Schilling's ERA impact:
Schilling's ERA standings points / League ERA differential
.188 / .075 = 2.51

Schilling gains the base team 2.51 points in ERA.

Now the challenge becomes condensing all these calculations into one formula. This is how it looks (this time I'll abbreviate):

(Base team ERA - ((Pitcher X's ER + base team's ER) /
(Pitcher X's IP + base team's IP) x 9)) /
ERA differential

If you're using the same cells I'm using, the formula becomes:

Formula for cell s13:
= (base team ERA cell – ((Schilling's ER cell + base team's ER cell)/
(Schilling's IP cell + base team IP cell) x 9))/
League ERA differential cell
=(o10-((m13+m10)/(k13+k10)*9))/s11

Ratio calculation for Player X:

Schilling's stats: 259.33 IP, 218 H, 33 BB
Base team: 1,080 IP, 1,080 H, 360 BB

Add Schilling to base team:
1,339.33 IP (259.33 + 1,080)
1,296 H (216 + 1,080)
393 BB (33 + 360)

Base team's ratio, adding Schilling:
(1,296 + 393) / 1,339.33
1,689 / 1,339.33 = 1.261

Base team's ratio after adding Schilling: 1.261

Schilling's ratio impact:
Base team ratio before Schilling - ratio after Schilling
Schilling's ratio impact = 1.333 - 1.263
Schilling decreases ratio by .072

Ratio impact of Player X:

Schilling's ratio impact:
Schilling's ratio standings points / League ratio differential
.072 / .018 = 4.0

Schilling gains the average team 4.0 points in ratio.

Condensed to a single formula, it becomes:

(Base team ratio - (Base Team H + Pitcher X's H + Base Team BB +
Pitcher X's BB) /
(Base Team IP + Pitcher X's IP)) /
League ratio differential

The formula for cell t13:
= (base team ratio cell − (base team H cell + Schilling's H cell +
Base team BB cell + Schilling's BB cell)/
(Base team IP cell + Schilling's IP cell))/

League ratio differential cell
=(p10-(L10+L13+n10+n13)/(k10+k13))/t11

14. Compute the total standings points gained by the first listed hitter and pitcher after entering a "TSP" column header in the appropriate row. In my sheet, this calculation will go in column "U" and the "TSP" headers will be in cells u5 and u12. This step is easy, and I'll demonstrate it on Mark Grace's numbers in my example. The formula:

Total standings points:

Total standings points for Grace in cell u6:
= sum(Grace's first category standings point cell:Grace's last category standings point cell)

The formula for cell u6: =sum(q6:t6)

Now, repeat the process with pitchers, using the same basic formula with only the row number changing.

Spreadsheet phase three: Entering all player statistics

At this time, project stats for all significant players in your league, if you haven't already. In the chapters ahead, you'll learn how to eventually use these numbers to value these players for your league.

1. Add in the statistics for all other players to fill out your sheet. Insert enough blank rows to accommodate all the hitters for which you projected stats in the last chapter and use the "cut" and "paste" functions to add the projections from your old sheet. Use the "insert" function at the top of your sheet and select "row" every time you wish to add a row. *Be sure to leave enough space or you will erase other data.* If you cover other data by mistake, there should be some sort of "undo" command from the "file" menu at the top to correct your mistake provided you do this before typing anything else. On most sheets, you simply need to highlight all the stats you need to move on the old sheet and select "copy," clear enough space on your new sheet, place the cursor in the new sheet on the first cell at the top left of the sheet where the new data goes, and select "paste" once the cursor is in the appropriate cell.

2. Copy the formulas to get standings point numbers for all players.

This step is simple -- just copy the formulas from the cells in the first row to the corresponding cells below until standings points are computed for all players. This is very easy, but if you don't know how to do so, simply consult your spreadsheet's help menu under the topics of "copy" or "fill." Your sheet should now look something like this (to save space, I've only shown stats for Arizona players):

	A	B	C	D	E	F	G	H	I	J	K	L	M	N	O	P	Q	R	S	T	U
1	Number of hitters:	14																			
2	Benchmark hitter								450	122				0.2711							
3	Base team								5850	1586				0.2711							
4	Standings differentials																8.5	21	5.5	0.002	
5	Hitter	C	1	2	S	3	O	PO	AB	H	HR	RBI	SB	AVG			HP	RP	SP	AP	TSP
6	Grace, Mark		x					1	298	75	7	48	2	252			0.8	2.3	0.4	-0.5	3.01
7	Durazo, Erubiel		x					1	222	58	16	48	0	261			1.9	2.3	0.0	-0.2	3.99
8	Colbrunn, Greg		x					1	171	57	10	27	0	333			1.2	1.3	0.0	0.9	3.35
9	Spivey, Junior			x				2	528	162	16	78	11	307			1.9	3.7	2.0	1.5	9.08
10	Cintron, Alex			x				2	75	16	0	4	0	213			0.0	0.2	0.0	-0.4	-0.17
11	Counsell, Craig				x	x		m	436	123	2	51	7	282			0.2	2.4	1.3	0.4	4.32
12	Williams, Matt				x			s	215	56	12	40	3	260			1.4	1.9	0.5	-0.2	3.68
13	Donnells, Chris				x			s	80	19	3	16	0	238			0.4	0.8	0.0	-0.2	0.89
14	Womack, Tony					x		3	590	160	5	57	29	271			0.6	2.7	5.3	0.0	8.58
15	Gonzalez, Luis						x	o	524	151	28	103	9	288			3.3	4.9	1.6	0.7	10.54
16	Finley, Steve						x	o	505	145	25	89	16	287			2.9	4.2	2.9	0.6	10.73
17	McCracken, Quinton						x	o	349	108	3	40	5	309			0.4	1.9	0.9	1.1	4.25
18	Dellucci, Dave						x	o	229	56	7	29	2	245			0.8	1.4	0.4	-0.5	2.07
19	Bautista, Danny						x	o	154	50	6	23	4	325			0.7	1.1	0.7	0.7	3.22
20	Little, Mark						x	o	130	27	0	7	2	208			0.0	0.3	0.4	-0.7	0.01
21	Miller, Damian	x						c	297	74	11	42	0	249			1.3	2.0	0.0	-0.5	2.77
22	Barajas, Rod	x						c	154	36	3	23	1	234			0.4	1.1	0.2	-0.5	1.16
23	Moeller, Chad	x						c	105	30	2	16	0	286			0.2	0.8	0.0	0.1	1.13
174																					
175	Number of pitchers:	9																			
176	Benchmark pitcher								135	135	63	45	4.20	1.333							
177	Base team								1080	1080	504	360	4.20	1.333							
178	Standings differentials																3.5	5	0.075	0.018	
179	Pitcher						W	SV	IP	H	ER	BB	ERA	RAT			WP	SP	EP	RP	TSP
180	Schilling, Curt						23	0	259.33	216	93	33	3.23	0.96			6.6	0	2.5	4.0	13.08
181	Johnson, Randy						24	0	260	197	67	71	2.32	1.03			6.9	0	4.9	3.2	14.97
182	Batista, Miguel						8	0	184.67	172	88	70	4.29	1.31			2.3	0	-0.2	0.2	2.28
183	Helling, Rick						10	0	175.67	180	88	48	4.51	1.30			2.9	0	-0.6	0.3	2.54
184	Anderson, Brian						6	0	156	174	83	32	4.79	1.32			1.7	0	-1.0	0.1	0.80
185	Patterson, John						2	0	30.67	27	11	7	3.23	1.11			0.6	0	0.4	0.3	1.26
186	Kim, Byung-Hyun						8	36	84	64	19	26	2.04	1.07			2.3	7.2	2.1	1.0	12.60
187	Myers, Mike						4	4	37	39	18	17	4.38	1.51			1.1	0.8	-0.1	-0.4	1.51
188	Fetters, Mike						3	0	55	53	25	37	4.09	1.64			0.9	0	0.1	-0.8	0.09
189	Koplove, Mike						6	0	61.67	47	23	23	3.36	1.14			1.7	0	0.6	0.6	2.90
190	Swindell, Greg						0	0	33	38	23	5	6.27	1.30			0.0	0	-0.8	0.0	-0.79
191	Morgan, Mike						1	0	34	41	20	9	5.29	1.47			0.3	0	-0.4	-0.3	-0.41

Save your work for now -- I will show you how to turn these numbers into player values later in the book.

Fourth Inning

Player values

We have established that a player's value is generally proportional to the number of points he gains you in the standings. Now, it is time to translate player standings points numbers to player values and, if your league uses a auction draft, dollar values. But first, you should be aware of the factors that determine player value, which I'll discuss in the following pages before showing you how to set up a value system that accounts for each.

Elements of value

Many owners I know go into drafts with a set of dollar values written down that they'll pay for players. Sometimes I will ask them how they arrived at their values, and usually the answer is that they're either arbitrary numbers or that they got them by averaging dollar values from several publications. Neither way is terribly accurate, especially the latter, because these owners don't account for all the variables that influence dollar values.

Value elements can be divided into "prescribed" factors, which are determined for you by your league's constitution or rulebook, and "relational" factors, which require some research and judgment on your part. They are ultimately rooted in your league's standings and the relationships that players have to one another.

The final arbiter of value is the much-ballyhooed pitching / hitting draft-budgeting split. However, I believe that allocating a certain percentage to pitchers and another to hitters is a mistake, for reasons I'll explain later.

Prescribed value factors

These require no value judgment or opinion on your part as they are simply dictated by your league's rules or constitution. The prescribed value factors are:

1. The number of teams in your league

2. The salary cap for each team

3. The number of hitters on active rosters

4. The number of pitchers on active rosters

These factors determine value because they establish which (and how many) players belong in your league and how much money is available to pay for those players. You need to do nothing more with these factors other than plug them into your value system.

Relational value factors

The next three factors are determined by relationships of how much players gain you in the standings as compared to other players and to players at their position. Ultimately, all are dictated either directly or indirectly by your league's standings. The relational value factors are:

1. Standings point differentials

2. The draft pool

3. Position eligibility factors

I've shown how standings point differentials are a driving force behind player value. However, they can also work indirectly (as you'll soon see) because they help define the draft pool and the eligible players at each position, which in turn set value standards. Below, I'll discuss the role of the other two.

Most would argue that draft budgeting (in other words, assigning a certain amount of your salary cap to hitters and the other portion to pitchers) plays a major part in valuation. I do not agree with this, and will tell you why in a moment.

The draft pool

A player has fantasy value once he becomes worth of a roster spot on someone's team. And, of course, value is determined to the degree that a player helps (or hurts) a team in the standings.

From these observations, we can draw some basic conclusions:

1. If only players worth owning have value, then players not worth owning have no value. This is obvious, but it's worth a reminder because it's a cornerstone principle of a value system. If a player is not worth a roster spot, you will not be concerned with assigning him a dollar value.

2. Because value must have an origination point, it begins precisely at the point where a player becomes worth owning. In other words, minimum value must be assigned to the players who are least worth owning. So if the minimum you can pay for a player in your league is $1, it stands to reason that the worst player who is worthy of a roster spot would be worth $1.

3. Everything else being equal, the more value a player has, the more value (or salary) the player should command. This is generally true. However, as you'll learn briefly, it's possible for "player A" to gain a team more points in the standings than "player B", yet for player B to be more valuable because of other players in the pool.

Position eligibility factors

This is where things begin to get more complicated. When teams are required to fill rosters with players of a certain type -- for instance, most leagues require that teams have at least one player at every position on the field (for example, at least one catcher, one first baseman, one second baseman, etc.). So if there are ten teams in your league and each team must have two catchers, at least 20 catchers (2 x 10) must have value, and that the 20th catcher establishes a beginning point for value.

Suppose for a moment that you were to play in a ten-team league where each team had to draft two catchers and five outfielders per team, and no players of any other position were allowed. The draft pool would consist of 20 catchers and 50 outfielders. In this case, the 51st outfielder might gain you four points in the standings, and the 20th catcher might gain you but one point. Does the 51st outfielder have more value?

The answer is "no." Although the 51st outfielder would help more in the standings, there is no room for him on anyone's roster, and as we've already established, players must be worthy of a roster spot to have value. Therefore, you'll have to be wary of position-specific concerns when building your value system and later assigning dollar values.

Draft budgeting and the pitching/hitting split

For years, fantasy baseball experts have argued over the topic of draft budgeting -- in other words, how much draft money owners should spend specifically for acquiring hitters and how much to spend specifically for pitchers. In fact, the prevailing thought that owners should budget for each is so ingrained within the fantasy community that, like everybody else, I sought a definitive answer to the question as I begun writing this book.

Two years of writing and four drafts later, I realized I'd been focusing on the wrong topic. Instead of even pausing to challenge the validity of the debate, I was too busy working to solve the riddle. Should I set aside 65% of my draft budget for hitters in a traditional 4 x 4 league, or should that number be more like 50%? Or what if that number should change for one of my leagues, a 4 x 4 league that substitutes strikeouts for ratio?

The turning point came when I realized that allocating certain budget percentages meant that I could potentially be advising owners to pay more for players who helped them less. It is senseless to say that a hitter who gains a team seven standings points is worth $20 and a hitter who could gain the same team eight points is worth $15, but that's where setting a budget for each area often leads. How are fantasy teams supposed to win pennants by paying more for players who help them less?

So instead of plodding through the debate on draft budgeting and building a value system on a faulty premise, I'll proceed with showing you how to build a system that gets the most for your dollar.

The process of value determination

Now that you've completed the calculation of standings points for all players in your league, you'll begin the process of determining individual player value. The steps are as follows:

1.   Determine the pool of players who are worthy of roster spots. For instance, if a league uses 168 hitters, you need to determine the 168 hitters worthy of roster spots and how many points each will gain you in the standings. If your league is like most, the 168 top hitters by standings points will probably not be the 168 hitters who occupy rosters. This is because there are more talented hitters at some positions than others -- recall the earlier example on catchers and outfielders.

Therefore, the pool has to be adjusted to include the guys who fall outside the list of 168 best hitters, bumping hitters at strong positions and adding hitters at weak positions if necessary. The process continues until the final pool contains enough players to satisfy your league's roster requirements.

On the other hand, the pitching process should be very straight-forward unless a league requires a specific number of starters and relievers. The latter situation is not normally the case, and if it is, owners should follow the same scarcity procedures as they would for hitters.

2. Make adjustments for position scarcity if necessary, using the last draft-worthy player as a reference point for all player values at the same position. If players at a weaker position bump stronger players from the draft pool (such as the catcher-outfielder example), position scarcity exists.

3. Adjust all individual standings point numbers according to these reference points. Because you'd only want to pay the minimum salary allowed for the least-valuable players, we must set the value of the last player equal to your league's minimum salary. These "last players" standings point numbers determine the value of all other players. Standings points gained in excess of these players' minimums will be called "value standings points," or "VSP's."

4. Determine how many value standings points the league earns as a whole. A player's value is going to be directly proportional to his share of the total VSP pie.

5. Enter critical numbers that dictate dollar values. These factors include your league's salary cap, the minimum salary you pay for players, and the number of players who occupy roster spots.

6. Assign dollar values according to each player's proportion of the value standings point pool. Dollar values will correlate directly with relevant standings points.

Spreadsheet phase four: Value phase

At this time, re-open your spreadsheet to begin the process of assigning value.

1. Sort the pitching and hitting pools separately in order of their total standings points. If you do not know how to sort, please consult the help menu of your spreadsheet or find someone familiar with spreadsheets to help you. *If you're new to the spreadsheet process, I strongly urge you to save two or three copies of your spreadsheet so you'll have a backup in the event of a sorting mistake from which you can't recover.*

Make sure that when you sort, you tell the computer to sort by total standings points and to include all columns for all players. The best way to do this is to highlight all rows of player data, including the player names, positions, and stats. *Do not highlight the headings or any of the data at the top* -- you don't want that sorted in with the player data or it will cause a real mess. (If you do this by mistake, simply use the "undo sort" command.) When you are prompted for the sort criteria, tell the computer to sort by the column letter that corresponds with the "VSP" cells. *Be sure to do separate sorts for pitchers and hitters so that you do not mix the two pools.*

On some spreadsheets, you can sort by highlighting all the player data, going to "tools," selecting the option that sorts only the highlighted data, and then specifying which row you want to sort by (in our case, column U).

Note: To avoid confusion, I will not sort my sheet by standings points; instead, I will leave the players in the order in which I've always presented them.

2. Define the draft pools of hitters and pitchers. I'll begin with the pitching instructions because for most leagues determining the pitching pool is very easy -- you simply select the number of pitchers allowed on rosters for the entire league. If your league specifies a specific number of starters and relievers, denote them with an "S" or an "R" in the "PO" column and select the appropriate number of each.

When you have finished selecting the pitching pool, do not discard the pitchers who didn't make the list (you may need them later). Instead, do one of two things:

A. Insert a few blank rows between the pitchers who made the pool and those who didn't.

Or:

B. *Set the "row height" to "O" (zero) in the rows containing these players to hide them.* You can do this by going to the "format" menu, selecting "row height," and setting it to zero, or using the "hide" command within the "column" menu. Later, if you need to find these players, find the rows before and after the hidden rows, highlight them, go back to "row height," and set the row height to the normal level, which is usually around 12.

Once we work with the hitters, things can get complicated. The most difficult part of selecting the hitting pool is determining which players belong and which don't as judged by the league roster requirements. The easiest way I've found to do this is by following these steps:

A. Define the catching pool. We sort through the list of catchers first because it's the place where position scarcity normally exists. Scan your entire list of hitters from top to bottom. When you find a player eligible at catcher, enter "C" in that player's "POS" box (column "H" in my example). Even if a player is eligible at catcher as well as other positions, assign him to catcher. Do this until you have your limit of catchers for the league. (In other words, if 24 catchers must be owned by the league, put a "C" in the "POS" column for the best 24.) Highlight the last catcher's name, statistics, and standings points on your sheet.

B. Repeat this for all other positions required by your league. Starting from the players with the most standings points, mark the appropriate number of first basemen, second basemen, third basemen, shortstops, and outfielders for the league until you have exhausted each position.

You may put players who qualify for multiple positions anywhere, but you should probably put them at shortstop or second base first if they qualify there. Highlight the last player who fills each position in case you need to refer to these players later. *Do not use the middle infield, corner infield, or utility spots yet.*

C. Once you have filled the appropriate positions, go back to the top of the chart and work down until you fill all middle infield and corner infield spots. Most leagues designate slots for "middle infield," "corner infield," and "utility." Remaining second basemen and shortstops should be assigned the middle infield slot until all those spots are gone; the same goes for first and third basemen at the corner infield slot.

Highlight and italicize the last player to fill corner infield, middle infield, and utility slots because these players are important in determining dollar values. In my example, I'll denote these by "M" and "CI."

D. Assign the best remaining players to the appropriate number of "utility" spots. Most leagues have "utility" roster slots that can be occupied by any non-pitching player. Find the remaining players with the best standings-points number and assign them to the utility spots by placing a "U" in their "PO" column.

Do not assign a position in the "PO" box to players who do not qualify for the draft pool at this point.

E. Separate the hitters who belong in the pool from the ones who don't. You can do this by inserting blank rows or setting the row height to hide the players who don't belong, just as we did for the pitchers.

F. Sort the draft pool by position. This will allow you to look at the position groups together.

3. Determine whether position scarcity exists for pitchers. It only applies when owners are required to draft a certain number of starters and relievers. If the last player in one pool has a higher standings point value than the last player in the other group, the rules for scarcity will apply. If not, move on to the next step.

If it does, note the standings point value for the last pitcher in each group and highlight the cells of each player.

4. Determine whether position scarcity exists for hitters. Note the standings points for the last player at catcher, outfield, middle infield, corner infield, and utility. If any of last players at these spots has a standings point value of less than the last utility player, position scarcity exists at that player's respective position.

In my example, the last utility player is worth 2.003 standings points. The last middle infielder is worth 1.665, and the last catcher is worth 1.126, so scarcity exists at middle infield and catcher. This means that in my example:

- Catchers have value for everything they contribute over 1.126 standings points.
- Players listed at second base, shortstop, or middle infield have value for everything they contribute over 1.665 standings points.
- Players listed at first base, third base, corner infield, outfield, and utility have value for everything they contribute over 2.003 standings points.

If you do not have a utility spot or middle or corner infielder slots, value at each position will simply be determined by the last player at each position.

If the last player at every position group has a standings point value equal to or above the last utility player, you do not have position scarcity so proceed to the next step. If scarcity exists, go to step five and then skip number six.

5. *Add the column header "VSP" for "Value Standings Points" to the right of the "TSP" column header.* In my sheet, this will be in cells v6 and v29. Calculations of player value will be formed in column V.

6. *Determine value standings points if no scarcity exists.* In order to determine value standings points (and ultimately, value), we've got to subtract the numbers above from each player based on their position.

Pitchers

Simply find the total standings point value of the last pool-worthy pitcher and subtract it from the rest of the pitchers in the "VSP" column, which you will enter into the cell just to the right of your last individual standings point header.

The general formula for determining value standings points is as follows. In my example, Gene Stechschulte is the last pitcher in the pool, earning 0.92 standings points.

Value standings point calculation:

Pitcher X's standings point value - standings point value of last pitcher

Schilling's value standings point calculation:
Schilling's total standings points - Stechschulte's standings points
(13.08 - 0.92 = 12.16)

The formula for my cell v30:
= Schilling's TSP cell – Stechshulte's TSP value
=u180-0.92

Hitters

If position scarcity exists for hitters, skip to the next step. If not, find the TSP value for the last draft-worthy hitter and subtract it from the standings points of every other hitter. Make this calculation in the "VSP" column just as you did for pitchers.

7. Adjust remaining values for scarcity. I'll cover just the hitters this time. If you need to adjust your pitching pool for scarcity (again, this should only apply if you must carry a certain number of starters and relievers) you can figure out how to do it by following my hitting examples.

This can be done by using some simple commands to do it for you (step 6-A), or by sorting the pool manually by positions (6-B). Resort to "B" only if you cannot get "A" to work.

> *A. Use the "IF" function to find value standings points if there is position scarcity at only one position.* If you have scarcity at more than one position, move to step "B." Here's how an "IF" statement works:

- "IF" statements test a cell for a condition and apply a certain formula if that condition is true, or applies another formula it is false. They can be used by themselves when testing for more than one condition, such as when there is position scarcity just one position.

Here are the simple rules for formatting a two-condition "IF" statement:

I. Always begin with the "IF" statement, then enclose everything else in parentheses.

II. The first entry inside the parentheses sets the condition, which must always appear in quotation marks.

III. The second entry, which comes after a comma, applies a certain formula if the condition is true.

IV. The third entry, which comes after the second comma, applies another formula if the condition is false.

V. If the condition for which you are searching is a letter, surround that letter with quotations.

Here's how they look:

=IF(condition, apply formula a if true, or formula b if false)

You'll need to create a formula that reads whether the player plays at the scarce position (catcher, in my case) and assign either the value standings point formula for catcher or the formula for players at every other position. Here's the formula I used for Mark Grace, which I will copy to the rest of the hitting cells later. The formula for Grace's VSP cell in, as best I can explain in plain English, would look like this:

= IF (Grace's "PO" cell reads "c", subtract 1.126 standings points, otherwise subtract 2.003 standings points)

Here's how my formula reads in cell v6:
=IF(h6="c",u6-1.126,u6-2.003)

If you have position scarcity at just one position and the formula works, move to "step eight."

A. Use the "OR" function in conjunction with the "IF" formula should there be scarcity at more than one position.

- "OR" statements can be used when testing for multiple conditions, such as the case where position scarcity exists at more than one position. Here's how they work in conjunction with "IF" statements:

I. Begin with the "IF" statement, then enclose the rest of the formula in parentheses.

II. The first entry inside the parentheses establishes the first condition, which will be enclosed in quotation marks if that condition contains a letter.

III. The second entry inside the parentheses, which appears after a comma, applies a formula if the first condition is true.

IV. An "IF" statement appears after the first two conditions, and is preceded by a comma.

V. An "OR" statement, preceded and followed by an open parentheses, follows. This starts the process of testing for the other "excepting" condition.

VI. Another condition or conditions are established before closing the parentheses. If one or more conditions meet the criteria, you may place them together between the parentheses, separating them with commas.

VII. A formula is applied if the previous condition is met.

VIII. Another formula is applied if none of the previous conditions.

This time, we have to "nest" the formulas, testing for the first condition and then providing more "IF" statements if the first condition is not met. This formula checks to see if the player is a catcher, if not, it moves to see if he's listed as a second baseman (2), shortstop ("s"), or middle infielder ("m") and makes the standings point calculation (u6-1.665) if so. If not, it applies the calculation for all other players (u6-2.003). As best as I can put this into words, the computation for Grace looks like this:

= IF(Grace is a "c", subtract 1.126 standings points,
IF (OR (Grace plays 2, Grace plays "s", Grace plays "m"),subtract 1.665 standings points, otherwise subtract 2.003 standings points))

My formula in v6 looks like this:
=IF(h6="c",u6-1.126,IF(OR(h6=2,h6="s",h6="m"),u6-1.665,u6-2.003))

If you have correct values, enter your formula and copy it to the rest of the players on your sheet and move to step seven. Otherwise, move on to step "B" and use the following method:

B. Adjust standings points manually. Sort the players in the sheet by the "POS" column, then by standings points. You can do this on some spreadsheets by going to "tools," then "sort," and selecting the "advanced" feature. This allows you to use multiple sort criteria. You should now have all players grouped by position and then ordered by standings points. Count to make sure you have the proper number at each position.

Next, enter formulas in the proper cells that calculate appropriate standings point numbers for each player based on the standings point number of the last player in his position group. In my example, I would use the following formulas for the following positions in the "U" column, assuming that third basemen occupy rows 16 to 27; second basemen are in rows 28-39, and so on:

- Third basemen: in *cell v6:* **=u6-2.003** (copied through *cell v17*)
- Second basemen: in *cell v18:* **=u18-1.665** (copied through *cell v29*)
- First basemen: in *cell v30:* **=u30-2.003** (copied through *cell v41*)
- Utility players: in *cell v42:* **=u42-2.003** (copied through cell *v53)*
- Shortstops: in *cell v54:* **=u54-1.665** (copied through *cell v65)*
- Outfielders: in *cell v66:* **=u66-2.003** (copied through *cell v125)*
- Middle infielders: in *cell v126:* **=u126-1.665** (copied through *cell v137)*
- Corner infielders: in *cell v138:* **=u138-2.003** (copied through *cell v149)*
- Catcher: in *cell v150:* **=u150-1.126** (copied through *cell v173)*

Your chart now looks something like this:

	A	H	U	V
1	*Number of hitters:*			
2	*Benchmark hitter*			
3	*Base team*			
4	*Standings differentials*			
5	**Hitter**	PO	**TSP**	**VSP**
6	Grace, Mark	1	3.01	1.00
7	Durazo, Erubiel	1	3.99	1.99
8	Colbrunn, Greg	1	3.35	1.35
9	Spivey, Junior	2	9.08	7.42
10	Cintron, Alex	2	-0.17	-1.83
11	Counsell, Craig	m	4.32	2.66
12	Williams, Matt	s	3.68	2.01
13	Donnells, Chris	s	0.89	-0.77
14	Womack, Tony	3	8.58	6.58
15	Gonzalez, Luis	o	10.54	8.54
16	Finley, Steve	o	10.73	8.73
17	McCracken, Quinton	o	4.25	2.25
18	Dellucci, Dave	o	2.07	0.07
19	Bautista, Danny	o	3.22	1.22
20	Little, Mark	o	0.01	-1.99
21	Miller, Damian	c	2.77	1.64
22	Barajas, Rod	c	1.16	0.03
23	Moeller, Chad	c	1.13	0.01
174				
175	*Number of pitchers:*			
176	*Benchmark pitcher*			
177	*Base team*			
178	*Standings differentials*			
179	**Pitcher**		**TSP**	**VSP**
180	Schilling, Curt		13.08	12.16
181	Johnson, Randy		14.97	14.05
182	Batista, Miguel		2.28	1.36
183	Helling, Rick		2.54	1.62
184	Anderson, Brian		0.80	-0.12
185	Patterson, John		1.26	0.34
186	Kim, Byung-Hyun		12.60	11.68
187	Myers, Mike		1.51	0.59
188	Fetters, Mike		0.09	-0.83
189	Koplove, Mike		2.90	1.98
190	Swindell, Greg		-0.79	-1.71
191	Morgan, Mike		-0.41	-1.33

Note: If your league does not use a salary cap and instead does a straight draft, you are finished. The players with the highest VSP values are your most valuable players. Whether a player is a hitter or a pitcher is irrelevant. The higher the VSP, the better the player becomes.

8. Enter new row headings to use in dollar-value determination. Go to the top of your sheet and insert ten new blank rows at the very top. Then, in the far left cell in each row, enter the following headings in this order:

- "Number of teams:"
- "Number of players, team:"
- "Number of players, league:"
- "Salary cap per team:"
- "Total league $:"
- "Minimum salary per player:"
- "Value $:"
- "Total VSP's:"
- "Value $/VSP's:"
- "HITTERS" (this row simply serves to separate the hitting numbers from the other row headings)

When you've done this, also enter a blank for and a "PITCHERS" heading just one cell before the "number of pitchers" row; this will help distinguish them from the hitters.

9. Enter critical numbers for each of these headings. In the "B" column just to the right of those above headings, enter the numbers that correspond with each header. The first two calculations ("number of teams" and "number of players per team") are easy, as are the salary cap and minimum bid per player. Here's how to figure the other three:

Number of players, league:

Number of teams x number of players per team

On my example, I put this formula in *b3*:
=b1*b2

Total league $:

Number of teams x salary cap per team

In my sheet's *cell b5*:
=b1*b4

Value $:

Total league $ - (number of players, league x minimum salary per player)

In my sheet's *cell b7:*
=b5-(b3*b6)

We have not yet discussed value dollars. We've used value standings points to see just how much value players have, and now we'll use value dollars to put a dollar figure on a player's worth. It establishes a ratio between the dollars the league has available to spend and value standings points.

There's just one small catch: as you may remember, the last player in the pool has no value standings points. Because zero times anything is still zero and we don't want $0 players in the draft pool, we have to make an adjustment. Therefore, we must take a certain amount of money out of the draft pool to account for this and add it back in later. So if the minimum salary in the league is a dollar and 300 players can be drafted, $300 must be taken out of the draft pool.

10. Determine how many VSP's the draft pool earns. You'll need to know how many value standings points your entire draft pool earns. Here's how to make this calculation, which should go just to the right of your "Total VSP's" entry:

Total value standings points:

Sum of all hitting VSP's + sum of all pitching VSP's
=sum(first hitter's VSP cell:last hitter's VSP cell) + sum (first pitcher's VSP cell:last pitcher's VSP cell)

In my sheet's *cell b8*:
=sum(v16:v183)+sum(v191:v298)

Note: Make sure you include only the VSP cells for those players in the draft pool. For the purpose of this example, I have deleted the players who didn't make the pool from the sheet. I don't suggest you do the same in case you need to add them later, but just make sure that your formulas include only the players in the draft pool.

11. Calculate the ratio of value dollars to value standings points. In the last cell among the new row headers, you made an entry of "V$/VSP's:" which stands for "value dollars to value standings points." In the cell just to the right, you'll calculate the relationship between value dollars and value standings points (cell b9 in my example), which will determine how many dollars each player is worth.

The calculation is as follows:

Value dollars to value standings points:

Total value $ / Total value standings points

In my sheet's *cell b9:*
=b7/b8

12. Compute dollar values for every player. Enter the heading "$" in the header row cell just to the right of the "VSP" header cell. Then, in the first player's cell, you'll need to calculate dollar values. Values start in cells w16 and w191 in my example. This includes putting back that dollar per player we took out earlier. This is how it's done:

Dollar values:

Minimum salary + (player's VSP's x (value dollars to value standings point ratio))

In my sheet's *cell w16:*
=b6+(v16*b9)

Copy this formula down the page and you will have dollar values for all players. Here's how my values and value factors look (note that some players from previous examples did not belong in the draft pool and were thus eliminated):

	A	B	U	V	W
1	Number of teams:	12			
2	Number of players, team:	23			
3	Number of players, league:	276			
4	Salary cap per team:	$260			
5	Total league $:	$3,120			
6	Minimum salary per player:	$1			
7	Value $:	$2,844			
8	Total VSP's:	982.7			
9	Value $/VSP's:	$2.89			
10	**HITTERS**				
11	*Number of hitters:*	14			
12	*Benchmark hitter*				
13	*Base team*				
14	*Standings differentials*				
15	**Hitter**	**C**	**TSP**	**VSP**	**$**
16	Grace, Mark		3.01	1.00	$4
17	Durazo, Erubiel		3.99	1.99	$7
18	Colbrunn, Greg		3.35	1.35	$5
19	Spivey, Junior		9.08	7.42	$22
20	Counsell, Craig		4.32	2.32	$8
21	Williams, Matt		3.68	1.68	$6
22	Womack, Tony		8.58	6.58	$20
23	Gonzalez, Luis		10.54	8.54	$26
24	Finley, Steve		10.73	8.73	$26
25	McCracken, Quinton		4.25	2.25	$8
26	Dellucci, Dave		2.07	0.07	$1
27	Bautista, Danny		3.22	1.22	$5
28	Miller, Damian	x	2.77	1.64	$6
29	Barajas, Rod	x	1.16	0.03	$1
30	Moeller, Chad	x	1.13	0.01	$1
184					
185	**PITCHERS**				
186	*Number of pitchers:*	9			
187	*Benchmark pitcher*				
188	*Base team*				
189	*Standings differentials*				
190	**Pitcher**		**TSP**	**VSP**	**$**
191	Schilling, Curt		13.08	12.16	$36
192	Johnson, Randy		14.97	14.05	$42
193	Batista, Miguel		2.28	1.36	$5
194	Helling, Rick		2.54	1.62	$6
195	Patterson, John		1.26	0.34	$2
196	Kim, Byung-Hyun		12.60	11.68	$35
197	Myers, Mike		1.51	0.59	$3
198	Koplove, Mike		2.90	1.98	$7

If your league is new or holds no keepers from one year to the next, you have accurate dollar values at this point. However, if your league has keepers, you'll need to made adjustments for inflation. We'll discuss how to do this, as well as how to adjust your values in mid-draft, in the next chapter.

Fifth Inning
Inflation and Dollar Values

Its draft day, and you sit at the auction table confident and prepared. You've done your homework, figured dollar values for all players, and have already assembled a roster of decent, low-priced keepers before the draft. All you need to do now is draft some big-time power hitters and you're primed for a money finish. You figure that you can grab a couple of guys like Bonds, Pujols, or Beltran somewhere in the $30-40 range, either at value or a little below, and you're possibly on your way to a championship.

The draft begins. Bonds goes for $43, and Pujols for $42. You smile and think that because everyone's overpaying for the superstars, you should be able to grab a Scott Rolen or a Todd Helton for around $35, and maybe an Edmonds or a Chipper Jones for $30. An hour later, those guys are all off the draft board and on other team's rosters at higher prices than you anticipated, and now you're scrambling to buy $15 hitters who are worth the price you have projected on paper. What's worse, you're now kicking yourself because you had the option to keep Pujols at $36 and Helton at $33. Now, instead of having these players, you only have an empty feeling in the pit of your stomach as your title hopes pass you by. What went wrong?

If this has happened to you, you may have failed to account for draft inflation. Because other owners kept players at salaries under their projected values, owners had "extra" money to spend at the draft table. In most keeper leagues, owners keep several players at or below value every year heading into the draft. This can have a dramatic effect on player dollar values. If you don't account for this inflation, you're going to be using price projections that are about as useful as a bullpen of left-handed relievers against a right-handed hitting lineup.

In the pages that follow, I'll demonstrate three distinct advantages owners can gain by making inflation calculations. Using them, owners can make better roster decisions before they submit their pre-draft keeper lists and also be more prepared for your draft.

Finally, if you have a laptop computer, you'll be able to take a spreadsheet to the draft and account for any over or under-spending that takes place on auction day. You can literally see dollar values change with each drafted player, and you'll have a very good gauge on what you should pay for players as this happens. If you follow the instructions in this chapter and take your spreadsheet to the draft, you will have a significant advantage over your competition.

When to account for inflation and deflation

Conventional fantasy baseball wisdom has been that after dollar values have been calculated, owners should make decisions based on those values. Then, it is advised, an owner should see who is kept and how much those players cost in relation to what they're worth, and then make an inflation adjustment.

The problem is that there is often enormous inflation in a draft. Therefore, if an owner is making decisions about keepers based on prices that don't account for this, he can wind up in the predicament I described above. I recommend that before you submit your keepers for the coming year, find out which players the other owners will keep (or make an educated guess) and make keeper decisions based on the anticipated inflation. I'll describe how to do that in the remainder of this chapter.

Spreadsheet phase five: Inflation phase

1. Enter a new column to record salaries for kept players. In the cell just to the right of your "$" column header, enter "KEPT" (for "kept") to record salaries of the players kept prior to your draft. During the draft, you will want to use the "KEPT" column to record salaries of drafted players. I entered this header in my cells x15 and x190.

Enter the salaries of all players kept in your league now. This will be in column "X" in my example.

2. Enter a column to calculate draft-available value standings points. In order to calculate inflation, you'll need to keep a running tab of the money available for the entire league to spend as well as the value standings points for un-drafted players. The easiest way to do this is to create a column that reads each player's value standings point number and copies it to the new column. To the right of the "KEPT" cell, enter a "DSP" (for draft-available value standings points) column header. I did this in cells y16 and y190.

Here's how that simple formula works:

Formula for draft-available value standings points:

Player X's value standings point cell = player X's draft value standings point cell

In my sheet, I'll enter the following in *cell y16:*
=v16

Now, copy this formula through the rest of the cells on your sheet.

3. Delete the DSP entry for any players who have been kept so that you'll take their standings points out of the pool.

4. Make any necessary changes to the draft pool. If someone keeps a player that you didn't have in your draft pool, you'll need to put him in your sheet and bump another player. For instance, if someone keeps a corner infielder that's not on your sheet, move the player into the pool and delete the last player in. More than likely, you'll assign the player to a utility slot and delete another player occupying a utility spot.

You'll also need to change your VSP numbers when the draft pool changes. Simply find the standings point value of the new worst-player and subtract it from the necessary players' TSP numbers.

5. Calculate the number of kept players. I'll make this calculation where the "KEPT" column and "number of players, league" row intersects. In my sheet, it's cell x3. Here's how to do it:

Number of players kept:

A count of all entries in the "KEPT" column
**=COUNT(first hitter's "KEPT" cell:last hitter's "KEPT" cell) +
COUNT(first pitcher's "KEPT" cell:last pitcher's "KEPT" cell)**

In my sheet's *cell x3:*
=COUNT(x16:x183)+(COUNT(x191:x298)

6. Calculate the dollar value of players kept. I'll do this where the "total league $" row and "KPT" column intersect.

Value of players kept:

=sum(first player's "KEPT" cell:last player's "KEPT" cell)

My *cell x5:*
=sum(x16:x298)

7. Calculate the available value draft dollars. Do this where the "value $" row and "DSP" columns meet.

Value draft dollars available:

Value $ - dollars spent + (minimum player salary x # of players kept)

My *cell y7:*
=b7-x5+(x3*b6)

Note: We had to add in $1 per player to account for that base dollar in everyone's salary, therefore the entry at the end was necessary.

8. Calculate the value standings points remaining to be drafted. Remember to clear out the VSP entries for the players already taken if you haven't yet done so.

Value standings points available:

=sum(remaining VSP cells)

My cell y8:
=sum(y16:y183)+sum(y191:y298)

9. Calculate the ratio of inflation dollars to remaining standings value points. The calculation is just like the first dollar value calculation you made, except now you're dealing with only the inflation-related numbers.

Value dollars to available value standings points available:

Total value $ / Total value standings points

In my sheet's *cell y9:*
=y7/y8

10. *Make the inflation dollars calculation.* In the furthest open cell to the right of the column headers, enter the heading "I$," which stands for "inflation dollars." In my example, I'll enter headers in cells z15 and z190. Now, make the entry that calculates dollar values and copies it throughout the rest of your sheet.

Inflated dollar values:

Minimum salary + (player's VSP's x (value dollars to value standings point ratio))

In my sheet's *cell z16:*
=b6+(y16*y9)

Congratulations -- you've now finished your final spreadsheet calculations and are ready to dominate your league's draft! Here's how mine looks:

	A	B	V	W	X	Y	Z
1	Number of teams:	12				LFT	
2	Number of players, team:	23					
3	Number of players, league:	276			7		
4	Salary cap per team:	$260					
5	Total league $:	$3,120			$64		
6	Minimum salary per player:	$1					
7	Value $:	$2,844				$2,787	
8	Total VSP's:	982.7				920	
9	Value $/VSP's:	$2.89				$3.03	
10	**HITTERS**						
11	*Number of hitters:*	14					
12	*Benchmark hitter*						
13	*Base team*						
14	*Standings differentials*						
15	**Hitter**	C	VSP	$	KEPT	DSP	I$
16	Grace, Mark		1.00	$4	$3		
17	Durazo, Erubiel		1.99	$7		1.99	$7
18	Colbrunn, Greg		1.35	$5		1.35	$5
19	Spivey, Junior		7.42	$22		7.42	$23
20	Counsell, Craig		2.32	$8		2.32	$8
21	Williams, Matt		1.68	$6		1.68	$6
22	Womack, Tony		6.58	$20	$15		
23	Gonzalez, Luis		8.54	$26		8.54	$27
24	Finley, Steve		8.73	$26		8.73	$27
25	McCracken, Quinton		2.25	$8		2.25	$8
26	Dellucci, Dave		0.07	$1		0.07	$1
27	Bautista, Danny		1.22	$5	$3		
28	Miller, Damian	x	1.64	$6		1.64	$6
29	Barajas, Rod	x	0.03	$1		0.03	$1
30	Moeller, Chad	x	0.01	$1		0.01	$1
184							
185	**PITCHERS**						
186	*Number of pitchers:*	9					
187	*Benchmark pitcher*						
188	*Base team*						
189	*Standings differentials*						
190	**Pitcher**		VSP	$	KEPT	VSP	I$
191	Schilling, Curt		12.16	$36	$38		
192	Johnson, Randy		14.05	$42		14.05	$44
193	Batista, Miguel		1.36	$5		1.36	$5
194	Helling, Rick		1.62	$6		1.62	$6
195	Patterson, John		0.34	$2	$1		
196	Kim, Byung-Hyun		11.68	$35		11.68	$36
197	Myers, Mike		0.59	$3		0.59	$3
198	Koplove, Mike		1.98	$7	$4		

You may wish to hide some of the less critical columns (such as standings points earned in each category) so that the screen of data in front of you is not so overwhelming. This also allows you to see all the key numbers at once -- otherwise, you may not be able to view a player's name and his dollar value at the same time. To do this, simply select "column width" on any column of data you wish to hide and set the width to zero. Also, you may choose to round off dollar values to whole numbers to save looking at all the decimals.

Finally, I advise you to check your figures. Add up the dollar values of hitters to make sure they equal the hitting budget and do the same with your pitchers. With so many calculations, it's easy to make a minor mistake that can throw off your entire value system.

Using your spreadsheet before the draft

As I suggested earlier, anticipate inflation before you submit your keeper list. You might have a player you can keep for $30 who's worth $29 in a world with no inflation, but if you have anticipated that other owners' keeper decisions make the player worth $37 at the draft, he's now likely a player you want to keep.

Using your spreadsheet during the draft

Having an inflation-calculating spreadsheet at the draft should give you a big advantage over your competitors. As I said before, you can actually use it to calculate running inflation values at the draft -- to do this, simply remember to enter a drafted player's salary in the "kept" column and then delete his corresponding "DSP" entry so that his salary and draft-value standings points are removed from the pool of remaining players.

However, there are some sticky issues that come with inflation, and I'll have to admit I'm not quite sure how to handle all of them. I will discuss these issues in the next chapter, entitled "The Draft."

Spreadsheet note: After you're done, you may wish to insert one more column at the far left of your spreadsheet. You can use this column to track who owns each player. Make the column small -- instead of using team names, use owner initials or two or three-letter abbreviations of their team names. After the draft, you can then sort the hitters and pitchers by their fantasy teams, add up each team's totals, and calculate the projected standings.

Sixth Inning

The Draft

Now that you know what players are worth and what your team's strengths and weaknesses are, you're ready for the most important day of the fantasy baseball year: the draft. Draft well and you can almost assure yourself a spot in the money in some leagues; draft poorly and you're likely looking at a lower-half finish. In the next few pages, I'll outline some simple "do's and don'ts" of drafting a team.

Draft day checklist: What to bring

Draft day is almost always the most important day of your season, and you should be fully prepared. Here's what I recommend bringing to the draft:

- Your laptop with your sheets of team rosters and dollar values. If you do not have a laptop, make printouts of each sheet. If you're really hard-core and don't have a laptop, you can always bring your desktop provided you don't mind the trouble and have room for it in the draft room.
- A separate spreadsheet to use to track your team stats and goals. Leave the appropriate number of rows for hitters and pitchers and leave columns to calculate their stats. Set it up similar to your value sheets so that you can simply copy and paste stats of the players you draft from your value worksheet to your team sheet. Set the sheet up to calculate team totals, and below them, set your category goals (for instance, 250 homers or a 3.90 ERA) so that you may see how you're progressing towards those goals.

You may wish to enter a separate line to subtract the stats you accumulate from your goals (for instance, a line that subtracts the homers you've acquired from your target number) to track your needs as the draft progresses.

- Printed copies of all your spreadsheets, just in case your computer crashes.
- Your computer's power cord or a battery backup
- Scratch paper
- A pen or pencil
- A calculator (you may need it to do quick math or in the event of a computer crash)
- A reference book with previous year's stats. No matter how prepared you are, there are often times where it's helpful to have a reference tool for those last-minute bidding decisions.
- The latest injury reports. If you don't bring a printed copy to the draft, be sure and check the 'net right before you draft so you don't draft someone who just got hurt, benched, or demoted.
- Adequate food and drink. Drafts are difficult enough without the added distractions of hunger or thirst.

Get a good night's sleep before the draft, and by all means don't show up with a hangover. Most drafts last six to 12 hours and can be exhausting ordeals.

Drafting tips and guidelines

Please note that I use the term "guidelines" instead of "rules." The reason for this is that most of the time you should stick to these principles, but there are cases where you may need to make exceptions. I'll explain those later as well.

Use your value system as your guide, not your god

The value system you generated is mostly good for highlighting buying opportunities and preventing you from doing stupid things. Use it for a bird's-eye view of who's left on your draft board, to find bargains, and to determine how much you should pay for each player. Used wisely, it's a more powerful tool than anyone else at your draft will have, but also know that it's not the "end-all, be-all." There are some times when you should consider overpaying, and times you should perhaps pass on a bargain, and I'll discuss those kinds of situations later.

Draft value

There is nothing more crucial to a good draft than drafting value. Owners should come out of the draft with as much talent as possible, and the value-conscious owner sometimes must focus more on acquiring raw talent and less on category balance. This may cause a team to be overstocked in one category -- for example, a team may stock up on steals and neglect homers because steals can be bought more cheaply. However, the same team will have a surplus of steals to trade for power later. Everything else being equal, the team that comes out of the draft with the most value should have the best chance to win.

Drafting for value requires a couple of things: patience and a willingness to not get hung up on owning a particular player or group of players. For instance, you may love Carl Crawford and think he's going to be the best thing since Rickey Henderson. If Crawford is valued at $40 and the auctioneer is closing the bid at $34, then by all means you should place a $35 bid and grab him. However, if the bid goes to about $40, it's generally best to pass and save the money for the players not yet auctioned.

The frequency with which you'll be able to draft players below value, as well as the margins below value you get players, depends on how shrewd your fellow owners are. Usually the more competitive a league gets, the fewer bargains there are, especially among top-level players. I've seen fantasy writers recommend that you buy players 20-30% below value. From my experience, this is practically impossible to do with any regularity. In competitive leagues, few players who command more than an average salary can be bought at less than 80% of his value, and the superstars can rarely be bought at more than even a 10% discount.

If this is the case in your league, be prepared to pay up to full value for superstars and concentrate your bargain-hunting on mid-level players with big upsides. In any case, a word of caution -- don't get so caught-up on finding bargains that you leave your team without one or two superstars. It's very difficult to win a pennant without a stud or two. The best formula I know for winning competitive leagues is to pay just below full value for a few rock-solid superstars and fill out your roster by bargain-shopping everywhere else as much as you can.

By being patient and sticking to your system, you may not draft your favorite players or have a team that's top-heavy with superstars. But, you can take comfort later when you've drafted a strong roster from top to bottom while other owners scramble among the bottom of the draft pool to fill six or seven roster spots. While they're paying $7 for $4 outfielders, you'll feel much better that you spent the middle portion of your draft grabbing $10 outfielders for whom you paid only $5.

A final warning -- if it's difficult to make fair trades with owners in your league, be more conscious of making sure your team is well-stocked in all categories and a little less conscious of value. One year I stockpiled steals and saves because they were cheap and I finished in the middle of the standings. I simply couldn't trade my closers and speed merchants for fair value in the categories where I needed help.

Exploit inefficiencies

Nearly every league has at least one category of under-appreciated players who always go for less than they should. In one of my leagues, it's the prototypical #3 or #4 starter, who can sometimes be bought for just over half of his value. In another, it's the base stealers who snag about 20-30 bags a year and score 80-90 runs. I like to populate my roster with these guys and let others overspend elsewhere.

Don't be afraid to spend lots of money early, especially if bargains are generally available later

Many owners clench their dollars as if they were a life raft on the Titanic, worrying that they'll have too little money left at the end. If stars and superstars are consistently at 15% or more below value, grab as many of them as you can before the other owners come to their senses. You may miss a sleeper or two at the end, but you'll have a team full of stars while your fellow owners are wondering why they have three guys named Rey Ordonez and $30 leftover. As the saying goes, a bird in the hand is generally better than two in the bush.

Don't panic if you fill your roster with two or three players with minimal value

This rule depends on your league's rules regarding player movement and the general trading climate. If it's easy to release players and pick up free agents and you are able to devote lots of time to monitoring the free agent pool, don't worry too much if you draft an outfielder who will be lucky to get 100 at-bats on the year. Even if you can't find a permanent replacement, maybe you can add someone who's playing due to another player's injury, ride that player until his playing time ends, and then repeat the process with another player. There are always players in the free agent pool who prove worthy of a temporary roster spot.

If you make a lot of deals and your league allows unbalanced trades (trades where one team trades more players than it receives), you may be able to convince an owner to throw in a marginal player who's better than the worst body on your roster. Other times, you may be able to call a player up from your reserve list or minor-league squad to improve your roster as well.

The benefit to filling out your roster with crummy players is this -- instead of spending $3-4 to acquire a player who's only slightly better than a free agent, you'll have extra money to bid an extra buck for a superstar or a better-than-average player that you otherwise couldn't afford. The more your league's rules allow for liberal player movement and the better you are at picking up good free agents, the less you should worry about having a couple of guys with little value. You can always easily pick up a $3-4 player in a trade, but superstars are generally much harder to acquire. In many leagues, you'll never be able to get a Roger Clemens or Vladimir Guerrero if you don't draft him because their owners won't trade them. If this is the case, throw your extra bucks at the superstars and worry about upgrading your roster-fillers after the draft.

Think twice before dumping a category

Owners often decide to punt a particular category, usually saves or steals, before the draft. If your league has ten categories or more, this may be something to consider. However, those in a standard 4x4 Rotisserie league have less margin for error. The advantage to blowing off a category, of course, is using the money you would have spent in that area towards others. Maybe you can still finish in the top-third of your league by blowing off a category, but in order to finish first you must finish at or near the top everywhere else.

Instead of deciding to dump a category before the draft, try to leave a draft at least somewhat competitive in every category. Instead of blowing off saves, buy one closer and a couple of good setup men, wait a few weeks, and see what happens. If you can get a break -- for instance, your closer reels off a dozen saves in April or one of your setup men lands a closer's job -- you may be at or near the top of the saves category without spending enough in saves to significantly alter your draft plan. If it doesn't work out, you can always trade all your relievers for help elsewhere.

An excellent example of this is something that happened in the Granny White Piker's League in 2002. The Bart Stars decided to keep Eric Gagne, who was named the Dodgers' closer at the end of spring training, for $11. He then picked up Mike Williams for about $15 in the draft, just hoping for a middle-of-the-pack finish in saves. The two combined for 98 saves and the Stars unexpectedly won the category while barely spending more than 10% of their budget on closers.

Remember that inflation figures change drastically over the course of the draft

Generally-speaking, having a list of inflation-adjusted dollar values will give you a large edge over your competitors. However, there's one big problem: the rate of inflation changes over the course of the draft. A player with a base (un-inflated) value of $20 could be worth (if you keep a running tally of inflation) $25 at the start of the draft, $27 one hour into the draft, $23 the next hour, $20 three hours later, and $19 near the very end. Of course, you still purchase the same player no matter what the price.

There are also a number of other inflation-related issues that affect dollar values. These things can render your value system almost irrelevant at times:

1. Teams have specific needs they need to fill near the end of the draft, and few opportunities left to do it. If five teams need a power hitter and there's one legitimate power hitter left, you can just about guarantee that the player will go higher than his inflated value.

2. Its common for at least one team to have saved too much money. Quite often, one or two teams have over half their salary cap left while all other teams have spent 80% or more of their cap. At this point, you can bet that the cheapskate with all his money left over is going to bid like crazy on any player with a pulse. This, of course, can single-handedly wreck any bargain-hunting you may wish to do.

3. Teams can throw all their remaining salary at a player when they're one spot from rounding out their roster. It's possible for a team to have $20-30 with one spot to fill with no remaining players worth more than $5. In this case, a team will likely bid as much as it takes to get that player regardless of his value.

With all these complications, it's difficult to set hard-fast rules with regards to what you should pay, but here are some helpful hints:

1. Consult your list of un-inflated values when bidding. If the $20 base player has an inflated value of $28 at the time but is going for $20, then grab him without hesitation. Buying players at or near their base value becomes an even-better idea when stars and superstars are involved.

2. If there's a high rate of inflation, do not go over a player's inflated value. Because the inflation rate will decline later, you'll get less for your dollar by paying full-price at the peak of inflation. You especially do not want to pay peak inflated value for a player when plenty of comparable players remain on the draft board.

3. Anticipate. If there's a shortage of something you really need (for instance, saves) and just a few guys left who can fill that need, that's a case where you should probably pay up to full inflated value. If you can grab the player who fills your needs at this point, it may force your competitors to pay above inflated value for the next similar players. This leaves you free to bargain-hunt elsewhere while others are still worried about that specific need. But if there are plenty of closers left and you need one, drop out of the bidding once it goes past the 2/3 mark between his base and current value. Chances are you'll get better bang for your buck later.

Once you've observed how owners handle inflation-related issues over the years, you'll have a better idea of how to wisely spend your money. As a general rule, I don't like to pay more than base value for non-stars and roster-fillers. For stars and superstars, I pay something between base value and full inflated value, but usually no more than ¾ of the way between those two numbers. In other words, for a player with a $30 base value and an inflated value of $40 at that point of the draft, I'd probably bid no more than $37-38. I don't have a particular basis for this philosophy, it's just a comfort zone I've reached after years of playing in my particular leagues.

Recognize the hidden value of an injury

I often purposely fill out my roster with 2-3 players who begin the season on the DL for a buck or two because it allows me to acquire extra players. As soon as the draft is over, I'll pick up replacements for my wounded bodies and stash them on my reserve list. Then, when those players are healthy, I can pick between the better of the injured player or his replacement. If I'm really lucky, both players pan out and I can trade one of them for something else.

Also, consider the case of two statistically-comparable players, one who's injury-prone and one who is not. Let's suppose they both hit .280 with 20 homers, 60 RBI, and five steals in 400 at-bats; one gets 400 at-bats because he's platooning and the other because he misses seven weeks due to injury. The platooning player must be on a roster the entire season to accumulate those stats. On the other hand, the starter can be replaced for seven weeks with someone else. If your replacement-level player hits .260 with eight homers, 40 RBI, and four steals over the course of the year, you can add two or three homers, a dozen RBI, and a steal to your team's totals while suffering very little in batting average. Therefore, the player who misses time should be the more valuable of the two.

Seek an age balance on your roster

Young players are often over-hyped at the beginning of their careers, and many don't do well in their first crack at the majors. Even Hall-of-Famers like Mike Schmidt and Sandy Koufax struggled in their first years. For every youngster that sets the majors on fire as a rookie, at least two will miss. I've seen several owners have as many as a half-dozen of the best pitching prospects in baseball on their team at cheap prices in the same season. Almost without exception, they won't finish in the top half of the wins, ERA, or ratio categories. Don't avoid young pitchers altogether, but set reasonable limits of two or three per staff. Young hitters are not quite as risky but are often just a slump away from the minors -- just ask anyone who owned Peter Bergeron, Paul Konerko, Marquis Grissom, or Morgan Ensberg during their first seasons.

Likewise, don't over-populate your roster with the geriatric set. Older players often experience a sharp decline with little prior warning. Schmidt digressed rapidly at age 38 without much warning, and then retired six weeks into the following season. (Schmidt's GWPL owner that year, who paid a dear price for him at the auction, heard the news on the radio while driving. He was so upset he had to pull to the emergency lane of the interstate, stop the car, and regain his composure.) Historically speaking, players are not likely to have career years once they're 35 or older, and teams that win leagues are usually those who have several young players with unexpected breakout performances.

While there are no guarantees in baseball, you'll likely benefit most by balancing your roster with some young players who have breakout potential as well as some grizzled veterans who have established long-term performance norms. This helps protect you against the extreme risks that come with both player pools.

Situational and psychological strategies

The tips I gave above are all valid, but sometimes you need to make slight adjustments due to the circumstances of your particular draft. Here are some additional tips to apply in those special instances:

Play the draft cycles to your advantage

Drafts run in cycles. In my leagues, people concentrate on drafting power hitters or big-strikeout pitchers early in the draft. This may be the perfect time to pick up a closer or that sleeper outfielder capable of stealing 30 bases. I've seen many drafts where there will be a run on closers, and 4-5 will be brought up for bid within a 10-15 minute span. Once everyone is worried about having enough money to pay for Trevor Hoffman or Armando Benitez, grab a decent hitter or starter -- he may come cheap at that time. When it's your turn to introduce a player, go against the cycle and get a player you want while others have their minds elsewhere.

Don't get caught in a "scarcity panic"

Players often go for several dollars above their worth because they produce stats in "talent-scarce" categories like saves or steals, or because they're one of the last quality players left at a particular position. Veteran fantasy baseball players have likely experienced a draft where a $25 closer went for $35 (or perhaps more) because several teams needed closers and he was the last remaining option. The $10 catcher can go for $15 if he's the last catcher who doesn't hurt a team's batting average and can hit double-digit homers. To avoid the wrong end of a "scarcity panic," buy players like those described above early in the draft before a panic run begins.

Let's suppose that going into a draft, there are only four available players with a legitimate shot at 30 saves. You have decided that you need to add one more good closer to your staff. The first closer comes up for bid early in the draft, and is going at or below value. This is perhaps the best time to buy this player. The teams that need saves may get desperate and overbid later.

Here's a good rule of thumb: don't wait to acquire these unique players when one or two remain. People generally begin to panic and overspend when only two remaining players fit a particular bill. By waiting no later than the third player in the particular group, you decrease your odds of overpaying for a player you really need.

Make a list of overvalued and undervalued players and use it to your advantage

It's good to know which owners in your league like certain players and certain teams, and which players are getting lots of favorable time on ESPN. For instance, there are several Braves fans in the leagues I play in, and it's inevitable that Chipper Jones, Greg Maddux, and Tom Glavine will all go for more than they're worth. One year an obscure player named Tuffy Rhodes went for several dollars more than he was worth because he'd hit three home runs on opening day and a few owners got really excited over the prospect of owning the next Willie Mays. Instead, he didn't quite finish the season as he'd started it and was playing in Japan within three years. I like to see these guys go early in the draft. It's a good way to rid owners of some extra dollars they might want when they're bidding against me on a player we both want later.

Likewise, it's nice to have an idea of which players might be undervalued. I always like to sneak these guys in at odd times like the beginning of a draft or when there's a run on a particular position or category. Often, I'll get them at bargain prices because everyone's stashing away money for superstars or focusing on addressing their particular team's needs.

One easy way to do this is develop a coding system on your spreadsheet so you may easily spot these players. Most sheets have the option to color-code cells by going into the "format" menu and choosing a color for that particular cell. I like to shade the cells of players who I believe will be overvalued red and those who are undervalued green.

Don't make huge bid increases unless the situation warrants

Sometimes an owner decides he really wants a particular player and is willing to throw out an unusually-large amount of money to scare others off. Don't make this same mistake. About once or twice in every draft in which I'm involved, someone will throw out a $1-2 bid on a mediocre player, and then another owner will make the next bid at $10-12 and buy the player at that price. Why would you want to do this and ruin any chance of getting him at $4-5?

There is one exception to this rule, and that's in the case of filling your last roster spot. Let's say you have $8 left and one pitching spot to fill. You throw out the name of some flame-throwing phenom who you really like and you know that another owner is also targeting this player. If the other owner's maximum bid is also $8, it may be wise to bid $8 as quickly as possible. This insures that the other guy doesn't bid $8 before you do and lock you out of the bidding. This is also one case where you shouldn't worry too much about overbidding for a player unless you play in a keeper league and want to keep his salary as low as possible for future seasons.

Use $2 bid increments at the appropriate time

If used properly, bidding in $2 increments can save you a buck on a player. Let's suppose that you have Edgar Renteria valued at $23, and there is at least one owner who covets him. Another has just bid $19, and you quickly bid $21. Either you get this player at $2 under value, or someone else will have to bid $22. If you had bid $20 and the other owner had bid $21, you would have had to pay at least $22 to get Renteria. Topping the bid by $2 in this situation has probably just saved you a buck or forced someone else to spend three dollars more than their last bid. This is a good way to scare off the owners who begin to break out in cold sweats once bidding for players reaches high dollar figures.

This technique can also cost you an extra buck, of course, but if you feel that you can get the player at that price by bidding an extra dollar, it can be to your advantage. It's best used against owners who are conservative in their bidding.

Try not to fill your utility spot or last pitching spot too early

Be careful not to lock yourself out of the bidding for players you want. This can happen when you fill your last pitcher's spot or last utility slot for hitters. If you are really fond of a particular pitcher or two but have only one pitching roster spot left, don't acquire an $8 pitcher for $4 when there are very good pitchers still on the board.

I made this exact mistake in 2001. I had a roster already stacked with good hitters and filled my last utility spot with a $31 for Edgardo Alfonzo, a star player who I figured would be worth about that amount. At that point in the draft, superstars were going for several dollars above value and I figured that I needed one more big gun to round out my roster.

About two hours later, I watched helplessly as the Bart Stars bid $2 for a young hitter named Albert Pujols, a player I had really wanted. By that time it was too late -- I had filled all my infield and utility spots. I couldn't bid on the player who turned out to be the bargain of the decade. To make things worse, Alfonzo had an injury-filled year and was only worth about $10 while Pujols hit 37 homers, knocked in 130 runs, and hit .329. This not only probably cost me the league title (I finished third), but Bart still has Pujols on his roster at a bargain price. Meanwhile, Alfonzo has become a run-of-the-mill third baseman and is long-gone from my roster.

Don't make a bid unless you absolutely want the player at that price

At many drafts there will be an owner who is obsessed with driving up the prices for players he doesn't want. You should not do this for three reasons:

1. You can make enemies in a hurry and other ticked-off owners will do the same thing to you.

2. It's hard enough to have a good draft without worrying too much about others' teams.

3. You may overpay for a player, or worse, get stuck with someone you don't want.

A good philosophy is to never bid for a player that you don't want at that price. Likewise, never throw out a player for bidding if you're not willing to own him.

Try to buy a sleeper or two early in the draft

In some leagues it's wise to introduce a sleeper for bidding early in the draft when other owners are preoccupied with drafting superstars. If you can get the first underappreciated player you want at a bargain price, try this again. Many owners sit on their sleepers until the end of the draft and wind up in a bidding war with three other owners who had the same idea. If you bring the player out early, you can either get him cheaply or target other players if you don't. Whatever happens, you likely stand to benefit -- you either get a bargain or you no longer plan your draft around a player or two you weren't going to own anyway.

Spend at least 95% of your time worrying about your team and not others

It's hard enough to draft your own team without worrying about other owners. Time spent focusing on opponents takes away from the limited time you have to address your team at the draft. Know how much draft money others have and which other teams might have similar needs in terms of positions and categories, but let that be the extent of your external focus.

Some owners really watch their competitors, hoping to pick up on body language that might shed a clue about what they're thinking. I would only suggest doing this only if you've mastered the draft process and you read others well. As someone who's done this for nineteen years, I've found that the advantage you gain may not be worth the cost of losing focus on your own situation.

Every player has his price

It's OK to follow your heart when you draft -- after all, this game should be about having fun. Just don't expect to win if you let your emotions control your actions. Don't stray far from the values you've calculated for players unless the situation truly warrants. If you want to own the Yankee rotation because you are America's biggest Yankee fan, that's fine -- just don't pay more than you should.

On the other hand, there are times when you should buy players that you don't like or feel are overrated in the real world of baseball. Though I've advocated purchasing high-skills players, I sometimes purchase players I'm not crazy about because their auction values fall so far below their projected values that they become bargains. Even in competitive drafts, some mediocre players fall so far below value that there's almost no way they can be worth less than what you pay. Even if your opinion of a particular ballplayer isn't positive, think twice before you let him go to your competitors at a price far below what you realistically think he'll earn.

Target players with talent who were busts in their first year or two

Top rookies get all the spring training media hype and consequently often go for relatively high draft prices. These same guys often fail in their first year or two but eventually get it together and succeed. But after a couple of failures, they're often all-but-forgotten by the media and your fellow owners, except for those who were once burned by them and vow never to own them again. It's not uncommon to buy a player or two fitting this description for $2-3 and receive a $20 season in return; Morgan Ensberg, Paul Konerko, and Marquis Grissom are great examples of this.

Near the end of the draft, shift your focus towards filling needs

Value is always an important issue, but the ultimate goal is to win. If it's the end of the draft and you need steals but have plenty of power, you should probably pass on the $5 catcher with double-digit home run potential and take the $3 outfielder who might steal a dozen bases instead.

If you're playing for the future, draft as many superstars as possible

If you don't care where you finish in the coming year, draft as many "name" players as you can. Later, when other owners are trading aggressively for the stretch run, you can trade your stars for cheap keepers that will help you in the future.

Take lots of notes at your draft, including the time at which certain players are drafted

This helps you to anticipate trends for your future drafts. If owners overspend for power hitters in the first hour of the draft, note it. In some leagues, the first superstar or two goes at or below value. Then, the other owners start to fear they'll be left without the big-name players and the next ten players drafted go over value. Knowing your league's trends will help you to know the best times to bid on particular players.

You might also note the last owner to bid on a player you own. If you want to trade that player later, there's a good chance that owner may be interested.

Notes on drafting pitchers

Avoid overpaying for mediocre pitchers, and target "unsexy" pitchers at bargain prices

In most leagues, an owner can draft several decent pitchers for a buck or two who will be worth several times the cost. In fact, no matter how deep a league's draft goes, there will almost always certainly be pitchers worth owning that no one bothers to draft.

Bargain pitchers usually fit one of these profiles:

1. Middle-relievers with good ERA's and/or WHIP ratios who contribute a handful of wins and saves.

2. Fourth or fifth-starters on mediocre teams or good teams that don't play in major media markets, or;

3. #1 or #2 starters playing on bad teams.

Of course, you probably don't want to fill out your entire roster with $1-2 pitchers, although we'll later discuss a strategy that advocates spending a very low amount of your budget on pitching. You may purchase one or two really good starting pitchers and a closer or two and fill out the rest of your roster with cheap hurlers. Or, you might buy one Randy Johnson and two closers and fill out the rest of your team with pitchers for $5 with much-bigger upsides.

The one thing you don't want to do under any circumstance is load up on $5-15 pitchers who are no better than the guys you can grab later for a buck or two. Pitching is somewhat unpredictable, and you'll be better off saving those extra dollars for quality hitters or a couple of truly outstanding closers or starters.

One note -- it's much easier to find bargain pitchers in leagues that don't use strikeouts. Strikeouts are more predictable and so adding a more predictable category tends to even out pitching categories by reducing the fraction of team average pitching categories. If that doesn't make sense, consider this: in a standard 4x4 league, half the pitching categories are team-average (ERA, WHIP). In a 5x5 league, the addition of strikeouts reduces the fraction to 2/5. In 4x4 leagues, it's not uncommon to draft a team's fourth or fifth starter for a buck or two and get double-digit values, or pick up a $1 middle reliever who puts up terrific ERA and ratio numbers and might even land a closer's job by the end of the year.

Once strikeouts are added to the mix, a couple things happen. One, owners are now paying $5-6 for the same fifth starter because starters rack up more "K's" than middlemen. Conversely, the value of middle relievers goes down because they don't strike out as many guys as the starters. As strikeouts become a larger proportion of the pitching standings point pie and the team-average portion decreases, bargains among starters become tougher to find.

Draft pitchers with true talent

Look for pitchers who have K/BB ratios of 2:1 or higher and strike out six guys or more per nine innings. If a pitcher has a great season without good numbers in these areas, it's likely a fluke.

I will rarely own a pitcher, regardless of his past success or current role, unless he's got the proper talent for success; in fact, I'll sometimes pass on a pitcher listed higher on my draft list in order to take a more highly-skilled pitcher whose projected numbers are not as good. The reason: it's hard to consistently project a pitcher's exact stats with any large degree of accuracy. You never know if that middle-reliever will win three games or nine, or if that fifth-starter will post a 3.70 ERA or a 4.50 ERA. However, if you consistently stock your roster with talented pitchers, you're more likely to build a quality staff from one year to the next.

Consider using the "LIMA" plan

This draft strategy has been in-vogue of late for 4x4 leagues using wins, saves, ERA, and ratio. The brainchild of Ron Shandler, "LIMA" stands for "Low Investment Mound Aces" and advocates spending no more than $60 of a $260 draft budget on pitchers. The LIMA plan proposes drafting only high-skilled pitchers at bargain prices and spending about half of the pitching dollars on saves while drafting as few innings as possible. The plan often works because highly-skilled pitchers often produce excellent ERA's and ratios and owner can generally pick up enough saves between a closer or two and some middle relievers to do well there. In turn, you spend more of your hitting dollars than most of your competitors, allowing you to stock up on enough hitters that you should be able to finish near the top in all offensive categories.

Shandler's had very good luck with the LIMA plan and highly recommends it; the plan has gained in popularity in recent years. If you employ the LIMA plan, he suggests those in 5x5 leagues spend slightly more that $60 on pitching.

Notes on drafting hitters

Don't leave the draft without plenty of power

In the leagues I play in, power hitters tend to go for slightly more than they're worth. The reason for this is that the home run and RBI standings generally parallel each other -- if a team finishes near the top in RBI, they usually finish near the top in homers. Since a poor finish in homers usually means a poor RBI finish, owners in my leagues place a premium on power hitters because although you can do poorly in one category and still finish near the top of your league, it's virtually impossible to do poorly in two categories and still win a league. Don't leave the draft table without power, even if you have to pay full value for players to do so.

Don't pay too much for someone just because he's an every-day player

There are lots of players who hit eight-to-10 homers or knock in 50-60 runs, but it takes 550 at-bats for them to do it. These players are marginal offensive talents with little value, and once they lose their job, they lose that value faster than you can say "Nippon Ham Fighter." If you have a choice between an $8 infielder who's been around ten years and will need 500 at-bats to reach his projected value and someone who can reach the $8 mark with his 200 projected at-bats, strongly consider taking the guy who plays less. A talented part-timer can double your investment (or more) if he can land a full-time job.

Target players who contribute some in every category

In many instances, players who contribute a little bit in every category go for a little less than they're worth. The early-2000's version of Scott Rolen is the perfect example of this. At that time, he consistently hit 25-30 homers, knocked in 90-110 runs, and hit around .285. He also stole anywhere from eight-to-16 bases per year, but because people thought of Rolen as a power-hitting corner infielder, they mentally lumped him in with other power-hitting corner infielders – most of whom wouldn't steal more than five bags a season. Players who are seen as equivalents go for roughly the same draft price, and so owners drafting Rolen essentially got as many as a dozen "free" steals every season. If you can repeat the same feat with four or five players, it's like adding a top-level base stealer for free.

When bad things happen to good owners

It's possible to come to a draft totally prepared, make most of the right moves, and still have something go seriously wrong anyway. Drafts are unpredictable and full of events you can't control. While it's always easy in hindsight to see where you made draft mistakes, it's rarely so clear to see them at the time you make them.

As a general rule, the better and more respected an owner is, the harder it is for him to have a good draft. No one ever wants to make it easy for the preseason pennant favorite and other owners will usually go out of their way to make drafting difficult for the top-notch owners. Thus, it can be easier to rise from the basement to the title than it is to stay on top.

Sometimes, an owner might even make it his personal vendetta that a competitor not succeed. While serving as the league Commissioner, one of my rulings ticked off a fellow owner. The angered owner threatened to show up at next year's draft with the sole intention of ruining things for me because of my decision in that case.

If you have any personal issues with another owner, settle your differences before the next draft if possible. If you find you can't resolve your differences, take the matter to your league's Commissioner in plenty of time for the situation to be resolved before draft day.

Anyway, here's a list of common (and not-so common) unenviable positions that owners may find themselves in at a draft, and how to deal with each.

The "copycat" owner

All of us knew someone in high school or college who stayed out all night partying, didn't study for tests, and would look over the shoulders of classmates for answers during tests. Unfortunately, some of them play fantasy baseball, too. They're not ready for the draft or have little confidence in their own ability to judge talent, so they observe top owners as they bid to see which players they're going after. Then, they'll try to sneak in a bid at the last minute to win those players.

This can also happen on a bigger scale for a couple of reasons. Once an owner wins a league for a couple of years, he's established credibility. Other owners begin to imitate the successful owner by copying his strategies or bidding for the same players, figuring that the league champ doesn't win every year by bidding on crummy players. This can also happen when the other owners get jealous. Sometimes many owners will gang up on one owner to ensure he doesn't get the players he wants without paying dearly.

An owner who finds himself in either of these situations is in a very difficult position, especially if multiple owners gang up on him. However, there are a couple of tactics that you can use to regain some control of your destiny if this happens to you.

First, quickly run the bid up on several decent players you're not set on owning. If there's a $20 player that you don't really want, bid aggressively to $15 or so. This may create the illusion that you really want the guy and camouflage the instances where you really do want someone.

Second, begin the bidding very high for players that everyone covets. This accomplishes two things. First, it levels the playing field by insuring that if you don't get players at reasonable prices, no one will. Second, it takes the focus off you and throws other owners for a loop by threatening their draft plans. This puts them in a defensive position for which they probably aren't prepared. It also depletes the amount of money they can spend.

You own few good players and there are few quality players left in the draft pool.

In all likelihood, you're toast at this point, so decide which of two avenues you'll take:

1. Play for next year. Concentrate on getting good players and sleepers who can be kept at reasonable prices for the next year. If there are any superstars left, grab them at almost any price -- you can always trade them for future help.

2. Play for this year. The strategy is similar, except you're no longer as concerned with price. If you have $80 left to get eight players and there are only five guys worth $10 each, spend $15 on each if you must and use the few leftover dollars to fill out your roster. The object is to assemble the most possible talent regardless of price. Once you have only $1-2 for each player, take the those with the biggest upsides even if they're big gambles. It's going to take a miracle for you to be competitive anyway, so buy lottery tickets instead of savings bonds.

You can't get a superstar at a decent price.

You want to win with bargains, but you almost always must own a superstar or two to win; what do you do when you can't get any at or below value? If everyone's overpaying for superstars by $5 or more, buy one at a buck or two over value. I'm not crazy about this strategy, but there may be times when you're forced to; the alternative is probably that you'll need career years from several players in order to compete for the title. Remember, the league's overspending ensures there will be bargains elsewhere, so try not to overpay too much or too often. I only recommend this if your league has a history of overpaying for superstars and you can't acquire one without overspending.

Post-draft analysis

Once the draft is complete, you'll need to see how you stack up against your competition. Here are some simple things you'll want to do:

Create mock standings

On your spreadsheets that you used to project players, create a new column in which you'll enter the fantasy teams for every player. Go back and sort each list by team, and estimate year-end standings from your preseason player projections. You'll then be able to see your needs and which teams are your competition.

Analyze the league

Once you've completed mock standings, you'll know the strengths and weaknesses of every team in your league. If you have glaring deficiencies, contact other owners about making a trade immediately. There are some categories, especially the team average categories, where large differences are difficult to overcome after about 1/3 of the season. Don't wait too late to address an area of obvious weakness.

Seventh Inning

The Season

You've drafted your team, made a couple of trades, done mock standings, and now you feel that winning your league should be a breeze. But because no one's season ever goes as planned, don't think you can neglect your roster and still win. You need to not only watch what your team does, but also what other owners are doing with their teams as well. We'll start with your team.

Monitoring your team

You should always have an up-to-the minute knowledge of your players' roles and performances, but here are some other things to consider too:

Pay attention to the first two months of the season but keep things in perspective

Every year, these things will happen:

1. *Some poor players get off to torrid starts.*

2. *Some great players have horrible starts.*

3. *Injuries and other circumstances will result in temporary changes of playing time, giving playing time to players who won't get it later and taking it away from guys who'll later contribute plenty.*

In analyzing players whose starts are way out of context with their historical performance levels, ask the following questions:

1. *In the case of a player who starts poorly, is there an injury that explains the player's performance?* If so, is it a nagging injury like a bruise or a blister that's temporary? Or, is it a more serious problem like a sore arm or a partially-torn muscle that could affect him for the season?

2. *Is the performance due to scheduling?* Does last year's Cy Young winner from last year have a 5.50 ERA because all his road starts came in Houston and Colorado? Did someone who normally hits ten homers a year pick up three first-week home runs in Coors Field and an inside-the-park homer when two outfielders collided and knocked themselves out?

3. *Is the performance due to a change in playing time that won't last?* Is your league-leading hitter only buying playing time until Larry Walker returns from the DL, or your hot fifth-starter just filling out the rotation until a team's ace recovers from injury?

4. *Are there personal circumstances that explain the performance?* Perhaps the player had a death in the family that caused him to miss a few games and he's still grieving, or maybe a player is still adjusting to a new league or new team.

5. *Has the player become a substantially different player from past seasons?* Perhaps the player added muscle or lost weight, or maybe just matured or regained some long-lost confidence.

Asking questions like these and applying a little common sense can help you make sense of early-season happenings. As a general rule, trade a player who's playing over his head for a better player who's started slowly unless you find good reason that the previous performances will continue.

Don't obsess over standings points in the first three months

Keep early-season standings in context. Team standings points totals usually vary wildly in the first three months of the season. Teams can easily gain or drop three or four places in the standings in one day. You should be more concerned with your competitiveness within each category more than your standing. You may be eighth in homers in early June but only nine homers out of the lead. Analyze your team and the teams in front of you -- if you believe you can still finish near the top of the standings in most categories with the team you have, there's likely no reason to panic.

Every month or so, make new projections for where you think your team will finish in each category

Keep a spreadsheet with all players on your team and try to forecast their statistics for the balance of the season, keeping in mind the player's current performance level as well as past trends. Total what you think your players will do for the rest of the year, then add in the stats you've already accumulated in order to get your projected totals. Re-assess your expected finishes within each category and adjust your strategy and roster accordingly.

Pay close attention to injuries

Many major injuries start as minor problems. In 2002, I had three key players -- Josh Beckett, Ken Griffey, Jr., and Curt Leskanic -- whose "minor" injuries sidelined them for most of the year. Beckett missed half the season with recurring blisters, Griffey missed two-thirds of the year with minor knee and hamstring problems, and Leskanic miss the entire campaign with a shoulder problem that was only supposed to cost him a month. Pay attention to players who can't seem to overcome minor problems -- they can sometimes ruin a player's entire season.

Pay attention to changes in roles and playing time

This one is pretty obvious and easy to track. Also, pay attention to the minor leagues. If you have a mediocre player and his major-league team has a capable replacement in AAA, you might consider trading that player before he loses his job (and any trade value he might have had).

Be aware of major-league managerial changes

New management can bring tons of changes. Hitters may lose jobs or be moved to a different spot in the batting order. Pitchers may lose rotation spots or closer's duties. In addition, managers have different styles. Some like to run more or go to their bullpen earlier. If you own players on a team that changes managers, know that each player's value could change slightly.

When players are hurt, demoted, or traded to the other league, don't wait long to pick up replacements

How many leagues are decided by a homer, a save, or two or three RBI? In the case of hitters, even picking up a bad player is normally better than having an empty roster spot for any length of time. For pitchers, this is not quite as true, though if your team is in a 5x5 league, or a league that uses only one team average category (as in the case of one of my leagues, which eliminated WHIP and replaced it with strikeouts), even bad pitchers are sometimes better than open spots. Be aware of how each potential replacement will affect you in the standings, and if all replacements appear to hurt more than they help, don't fill that spot. Generally, though, it's better to replace players than keep open spots for more than a week or so.

Consider dumping a category if you have an irreversibly-poor start

Let's say its mid-May and your team is in tenth. You left the draft with a strong team but you've lost Manny Ramirez for the year and most of your other hitters have slumped for the first six weeks. Ramirez's injury has put you in a hole as it should -- almost no team can lose a slugger of that magnitude and not feel the effect. You know that the RBI and home run deficits you face can't be overcome without making a move. This is a good time to consider blowing off one category (probably saves or steals) to trade for a slugger as long as the net effect of the trade stands to gain you more points than it costs you.

If you're going to dump a category, I recommend a team-average category because they're often less predictable than their team total counterparts. You can try to dump batting average or ERA and still manage to finish with a few points because success in the category is not dependent on playing time unless your league has established at-bat or innings-pitched minimums.

Carefully monitor the free agent pool

Keep a list of the top three or four free agent hitters and pitchers you would pick up in the event of a roster opening. If your league's rules are liberal in terms of roster movement, always be on the lookout for free agents who are better than the ones on your team. If you can't just waive a player on your team at will to pick up a free agent you like, call another owner and offer him a two-for-one trade. This helps his team and frees a roster spot for the player you'd like to pick up.

Keep a special eye on any middle reliever who pitches well as his team's closer is struggling. There are normally one or two closers picked up from the free agent wire in even the most competitive of leagues most years.

Beware of impending disaster

This is especially true for young pitchers who throw more innings than they've ever thrown before. As pitchers approach a new level of workload, they often hurt their arms or tire. A recent example is Vicente Padilla, who threw 87 innings in 2000, 115 innings in 2001, and 113 innings in the first half alone of 2002. Padilla had a respectable second half but he was clearly becoming exhausted -- he threw only 93 innings the second half and his strikeout numbers per nine innings, which had been 7.4 and 7.6 respectively over his previous two full seasons, dropped to 4.8 in the second half. I owned Padilla in the second half of 2002 and felt more than a little lucky that his ERA was only 3.30 in that time period. His success was mostly due to the defense behind him and his knack for stranding base runners at key moments.

Use your free agent bid money wisely

Many leagues award each team a certain amount of free agent bidding money from which they can acquire un-owned players during the season. Under normal circumstances, don't blow too much on any one player as it is a long season. However, many teams make the opposite mistake and hold their bid money for too long.

When bidding for a player, consider his long-term impact on your roster. You obviously do not want to blow a large chunk of money for a roster-filler for one or two weeks. Also consider the length of time remaining in the season. The more time left in the year, the more you should spend for a player who can help you long-term, all things being equal. In other words, you get more bang for your buck purchasing the same player in May than you do in August. I would rather err by paying good money for a solid player early in the season than hoarding my money in the hopes of landing a superstar later. At least you know you're getting something for your money rather than run the risk of getting nothing later.

Monitoring the competition

Knowing your roster is only half the battle. Here are some other things you need to watch aside from your own roster:

Capitalize on another owner's panic

As I stated earlier, great players may get off to horrible starts and their owners sometimes panic. Call their owners and remind them exactly how awful they've been. This is a great time to acquire a player at a bargain price.

Pay close attention to trades within your league

Just as you need to change your player forecasts throughout the season, you should consider what other teams do and how that will impact the standings. If the three teams behind you in saves just picked up closers, you may need to do the same.

Make special effort to pass your competitors in as many categories as possible

If you're in a close race with another owner and trail him by a point or two in a couple of categories, attempt to pass him in those areas. Each time you can do this is like gaining two points – you gain one and he loses one, so it cuts your work in half.

Play defense by beating others to the punch

If you and a competitor both eye a particular player who another owner has on the trading block, get him before your competitor does. This makes it much more difficult for the other guy to compete -- now, he's got to get a player of equal value to the one you acquired just to cancel out your trade. This might discourage him from making further moves to improve his team and encourage him to play for next year.

Consider trades that take points away from your opponents

This is especially something to consider once you've exhausted all avenues to help your own team. If you've got power to spare, trade a power hitter to a team nipping on the heels of your competitor in homers and RBI. Whether you gain or he loses, it's all the same to you.

Watch to see if other teams are dumping

Teams who dump often fall like a rock in the standings. Therefore, your team can be affected by several points as a result of dump trades (trades where one team trades for the future with a blatant disregard for the present), regardless of whether you're involved. Even if you have a safe lead over your competitors, they can often get back in contention as others ahead of them sink to the bottom.

When other teams start dumping, act quickly

Once a team dumps, other teams react as a shark would to blood. Wait long, and all the goodies will be gone.

If you decide to dump, don't wait until it's too late

You should never hit the panic button in mid-May if your team still has a reasonable shot to finish in the money. But if your team is in last place after a month or two and your three biggest superstars have been DL'd for the season, it's probably time to think about the future. No matter how bad your team, you probably have at least one or two players that other owners covet. Often times, when one team decides to pack it up for the year, one or two other teams will follow. If your team's outlook is so dismal that you have no chance at a top-half finish, don't wait until other teams have traded for all the good available keepers before you make a move. Everything else being equal, the first team that dumps usually gets the best prospects in return.

Use "football fever" to your advantage

Many die-hard sports fans play both fantasy football and fantasy baseball. With there being some overlap in the two seasons, you may gain a competitive advantage as the NFL season gets closer just by paying attention. Most fantasy football players have their drafts in mid-to-late August, and football season normally kicks off about the first or second week of September. This is just about the same time that the rules allow MLB teams to expand their rosters to 40 players, and most call up their stud minor-leaguers for a short audition.

This is the perfect time to distract your fellow owners. Check out the online editions of the hometown papers of their favorite teams, and send them links to training camp reports. Engage them in discussion on how their team might do. Ask them who win the starting quarterback job as camp breaks. The more you can get them to think about football, the better chance you'll have of calling up a hot prospect or making a key waiver claim your competitors might have missed.

Other in-season notes

Read the news with healthy skepticism

If a manager says disparaging things about a particular player or threatens to bench him, consider that there may be a ulterior motive involved. Some players respond better to a kick in the pants than anything else, so a manager may threaten to platoon a slacking outfielder with hopes that his quote hits the paper and motivates the player.

Be especially cautious when dealing with closers. Inevitably, all but the very best closers struggle through rough patches during a season and managers talk about giving other pitchers a chance. This usually sends minor shock waves throughout fantasy leagues, with fantasy owners picking up every available and reasonably-good arm from their free agent list off that player's ML team. More often than not, the struggling pitcher gets his act together and keeps his job.

There are many times when a manager means what he says, but always keep his comments in perspective. If Mike Scoscia threatens to bench Vladimir Guerrero for Chone Figgins, you can be reasonably-certain it won't happen for more than a game or two.

Dissecting trade rumors

Inevitably, one or more of your players will be the subject of trade rumors throughout the season. This is especially disconcerting if your league doesn't allow you to keep players who move to the other league and one of your Mets is rumored to become a Yankee any day.

The good news is that, from my experience, most trade rumors never come to fruition. The bad news is that a large number of trades happen without any forewarning. I once lost three good players in the span of a month, none of whom were expected to go anywhere up until the moment of the trade.

When you do hear a trade rumor, examine what might be the underlying cause. If the player will be a free agent at the end of the season and his team is out of contention, he's a prime trade target. If the player is underachieving or taking a high salary and there's a potential replacement on the bench or in the minors, be cautious as well. If the player is just a general pain-in-the-butt, he might also be a candidate to be moved. The

Indians shipped Milton Bradley to the Dodgers just before the start of the 2004 season because he'd become more trouble than he was worth.

Furthermore, most deals occur on or right before the July 31 major-league trading deadline. This means that even if you lose a player, you still stand to get four months of stats from him anyway.

Seventh Inning Stretch

Rules, stat services, Commissioner duties, and having fun

In this chapter, we'll take a break from the world of dollar values, projections, and scouting to look at some other fantasy baseball-related topics such as commissioner duties, rules suggestions, and stat services. And, since fantasy baseball should also be about having fun (while winning, of course!) I've enclosed some anecdotes and suggestions on how to make your league more interesting as well.

Rating the Statistical Services

Unless you're either really cheap, stuck in the Stone Age, or have a particularly gracious Secretary or Commissioner in your league who doesn't mind doing stats by hand, your league probably utilizes a stat service to calculate league standings. Here is a quick review of some of the major stat services, each rated for both quality of service and value.

All-Star Stats
allstarstats.com
Quality: Four stars
Value: Two and one-half stars
All-Star Stats is affiliated with Rotoworld.com and offers comprehensive statistical and Commissioner services across the four major sports. Rotoworld's strengths are these: they can track nearly every stat you wish, they generate timely statistics on a daily basis (standings through the previous day are usually calculated by 7:00 AM Eastern the following morning), they link nicely with Rotoworld so that you can easily follow your players, and probably the best feature, their service allows

teams to place free agent bids on-line so that other owners don't know what other teams bid until the bidding period is expired. This is especially nice if your league's Commissioner supervises the free agent bidding and is bidding on players himself. It removes any conflict of interest that may exist and far less taxing on the league officers as well.

On the whole, All-Star Stats offers excellent options and is designed to handle most fantasy leagues no matter what the categories or scoring methods are. I don't think they're a great value, however. They do a good job, but unless you need someone to handle free agent bidding, you can find an equally-good service for much cheaper. In the Cool Papa Bell League, we also had a bad experience when All-Star Stats didn't follow orders from our Commissioner. Their inattention to detail then caused a major problem with the integrity of our free agent bidding. I can accept the fact that people are human and make mistakes, but unfortunately the company never offered a partial refund or even an apology. That's a bitter pill to swallow when your league pays hundreds of dollars a year for service.

CBS Sportsline's Commissioner.com
Commissioner.com
Quality: Three and one- half stars
Value: Five stars

Commissioner.com is sometimes complicated to navigate, a little slow, and their transaction and Commissioner services leave a lot to be desired. There is no system in place for free-agent bidding, so that's a major headache for the Commissioner. But at ten bucks a team, you can't beat the price, and that's why I have no qualms about recommending their service to most fantasy owners. They also get high marks for reporting flexibility, as you can see league, team, or player stats in almost any form for most any time period you prefer.

Yahoo!'s Commissioner Service
sports.yahoo.com

I've never used Yahoo!'s stat services for a traditional fantasy league, though I have used them for a head-to-head league and they were fine. Yahoo!'s prices and services vary according from one type of league to another.

Other services

I've not used or reviewed any of them, but here are some other companies for your perusal:

UsaStats.com

CustomStat.com

SportsVoice.com

Being the Commissioner

There's no more challenging task in fantasy baseball than serving as your league's Commissioner. In some leagues with difficult personalities, it's a no-win situation. The Commissioner can often be accused of showing favoritism to himself or his friends. Things can get especially heated in leagues where large sums of money are involved.

I've seen it suggested in many a fantasy baseball book or column that you select a person not involved in your league to be the Commissioner, as if people are just dying to spend hours of their free time involved in a no-win situation where they have no vested interest. Since this is not realistic, most of us have to select someone from within to do the dirty work.

Because it's a thankless job, I would suggest making life on your Commissioner as easy as possible. Here are some ways to do this:

1. Split the Commissioner's duties into several parts. Our league currently has four people responsible for running the league -- the Commissioner, who tracks all transactions and league rosters; the Assistant Commissioner, who is in charge of preparing the list of the auction's draft pool; the Auctioneer, who simply runs the auction; and the Treasurer, who collects and keeps track of money.

2. Cut your Commissioner a financial break for playing. We charge a fixed entry fee to participate in our league. This covers auction money as well as free-agent call-ups and the stat service charge. We usually let our Commissioner play for free or dramatically reduce his fees. It's still as if we're paying him about a third of minimum wage for his time and trouble, but it's something.

Finally, if you happen to be the lucky one to be the Commissioner, here's the "golden rule" of Commissionership: be fair, consistent, and exercise common sense in all your dealings. Some people choose to wield power like an iron fist, allowing nary an exception to the owner who was ten seconds too late in activating his player for the day's game. Others take a more relaxed approach, knowing we're all bound to goof something up at one point or another. Choose one approach or the other, but communicate your philosophy to everyone and treat all owners with equal respect.

Your league's ownership

Each league has its own personality. Some leagues are casual groups of friends where the competition isn't as important as the excuse to spend time with one another. Others play for prize pools worth tens of thousands of dollars in a cut-throat competition from start to finish.

The best way to have a solid, unified league is to decide what you're all about. If you're all in it to be buddies more than anything, don't bring in divisive personalities or the win-at-all-costs owner. If you're all super-serious, don't invite your fly-by-the-seat-of-his-pants buddy who may, or may not, show up for the draft depending on his mood that day.

Knowing what you want to be saves your league a lot of trouble and headaches -- believe me, at times our league has learned the hard way.

Your league's rules

The original founding fathers of Rotisserie ™ Baseball prescribed a set of rules twenty years ago than many leagues still use today. While I think the founding fathers were on the right track, here are some variations from their rules that may be worth your consideration:

Allow relief for the owner who loses traded players

The original Rotisserie ™ rules stated that if a player was traded to the other league, his owner lost that player. Many leagues still stick to that rule, but I'm a strong advocate of compensating teams who lose players to the other league for a number of reasons:

1. It rewards skill rather than luck. There will always be a certain amount of luck in fantasy baseball, but this rule helps insure that the best teams win instead of the luckiest teams. I once had a stretch in an NL-only league in which I lost five key players to the American League in about a 12-month span, and each time I had to replace those guys with players who weren't as good as the guys I lost. It's disheartening to build a championship-level club only to lose the title because you had key players traded and your competitors didn't.

2. In deep leagues, the replacement-level players contribute little-to-nothing. In the GWPL last year (where owners can't keep guys traded to the other league), one owner lost Cliff Floyd to the AL and his best choices for replacement were Lenny Harris and Joe McEwing. In real baseball, once a team trades a 600-at bat player, they plug in guys to replace the traded player and don't lose any at-bats as a team. In deep leagues, fantasy owners lose 600 at-bat-per-season players and replace them with 150 at-bat players. It doesn't even out.

One way to help teams who lose players is to let them keep the statistics of players who change leagues. We're more technologically-advanced than we were at the time of the founding fathers. When Rotisserie ™ Baseball was introduced, Commissioners calculated stats by hand from papers like *The Sporting News* and *USA Today*. Finding stats for players in the other league was simply more trouble for the Commish, but now most leagues use stat services and it's no trouble to track stats for traded players. Perhaps this was a reason for the original rule.

If you adopt this suggestion, consider going to a "closed system" whereby players traded over from the other league are not eligible to be picked up. This helps maintain a statistical balance so that two players (the one traded and the one who came over) are not accumulating stats in your league.

If you're not crazy about that solution, consider this one: allow those who lose players to have the salary of their lost player added to their free-agent bidding cap beyond certain salary amounts. (The salary limitations have to be put in place because you don't want someone who loses a player of minimal value to gain a bidding advantage.)

In our league, each team has $100 of free agent bid money per season with a $90 maximum bid for one player. Teams usually save most of their bid money to spend on the one AL stud who switches leagues, so a bid of anything less that $90 will not get that player. So here's how we help the unfortunate owners who lose players: owners losing players with a salary over $10 may add the portion over $10 of the lost player's salary to their maximum bid. So, when a $25 Octavio Dotel was traded to the Oakland A's in 2004, the Bart Stars had their free agent bid cap raised to $115 with a maximum bid of $105. This meant that Bart was able to pick a talented player as compensation for Dotel at some point in the year.

If there is a second instance within the same season of a team losing a player over $10, that team gets another $90 added to their bidding cap plus the portion of that player's salary over $10. This ensures that every time a team loses a player of value, there is some compensation in return.

Allow for September special reserves

Many leagues do not allow for player replacement unless a player is DL'd or sent to the minors. Unfortunately for fantasy players, major league clubs almost never disable or demote players in September. So if a key player on your team goes out on September 1 and you can't reserve or release him, you're up the creek. Furthermore, most fantasy leagues have trade deadlines that expire before September. In this case, there's not a thing you can do to replace those players. Several years ago, the GWPL's Lee Press-On Nails lost an eight-point lead in the final week when Larry Walker and a slew of other key players sat out the final dozen games or so due to injury. The Nails lost their long-held lead – and the title -- on the last day of the season. If the Nails just had some of those guys get an at-bat every now and then, they would have won. This prompted our rule change, which has now been in effect for almost a decade.

We allow owners to reserve one hitter and one pitcher in September for any reason, the only catch being that once the player is reserved he can't be re-activated. We instituted the rule several years ago and no one's complained since.

Consider switching to 5x5

If you're in a traditional 4x4 league, you probably don't use runs scored or strikeouts. This means that staff workhorses and leadoff hitters probably have less value in your league than they do in real baseball. I've played in both types of leagues and find that player value in real baseball typically mirrors 5x5 leagues more so than 4x4 leagues. The downside is that you have more stats to keep up with, but if you're a baseball purist it's probably worth the switch.

Allow a "special waive" each half of the season

If you're an owner playing in a league with restricted roster movement, there are a few times every year where you hope you have an injury or a minor-league demotion so you may call up a certain player from the free-agent pool. Other times, a starting pitcher may be wrecking your ERA and WHIP but his ML team keeps throwing him to the wolves every fifth day. The GWPL allows teams to waive players for any reason, once before the all-star break and once after the break. This rewards shrewd owners who aren't lucky enough to have roster openings when they need them.

Consider changing your league's salary structure

Some leagues allow owners to keep players at the same price for up to three years. Others don't allow players to be kept from year to year. Both extremes can contribute to league apathy. The first system makes it easier for owners to build dynasties, and a really good owner can virtually lock up a league title for two or three seasons before the draft even occurs. The second causes owners to completely lose interest as their team drops out of the race.

The GWPL has a salary structure that works so well that it's remained unchanged for nineteen years. Here's how it works:

- Players valued at $1-4 may be kept the next year at $5.
- Players valued at $5-9 may be kept the next year at $10.
- Players valued at $10 or more may be kept the next year at a 10% raise rounded to the nearest dollar. Numbers ending in a "five" are rounded to the highest dollar (in other words, a $35 player would be $39 the next season).
- Long-term contracts work as follows: owners determine the number of years to which they wish to sign a player, multiply that number by $5, and add the original salary. If you wish to sign a $2 player to a three-year deal, he would be $17 each year for the next three seasons ($2 + $5 + $5 + $5). Once a player is in a long-term deal, the owner has to pay that player's salary for the duration of the contract unless the player is traded to the other league, in which case the contract is terminated. If the owner wishes to release the player, his auction salary cap is reduced by that player's salary for every year in which he should have been under contract. After the last year of the contract, the owner has a non-binding option to keep the player for one more year at a 10% raise.

This system strikes a fair balance between the extremes I described above. In fact, it's brought such competitive balance that we've had seven different champions in the last seven seasons.

And just for fun...

Many leagues have unique traditions that make their leagues more fun. In the Granny White Pikers' League, we give an annual Steve Howe Award, named for the former Yankees/Dodgers/Twins/Rangers hurler who, err... couldn't quite keep his nose clean. We give the Howe Award every year to the owner of the first player to commit a grievous violation of the law, which can be anything from with being busted in a compromising position with a 16-year old to getting caught with an illegal substance.

This idea was the twisted brainchild of Brennan McGehee and Steven Edwards, who collect a buck or two from each owner who wishes to participate in the race for the Howe Award. The Howe Award usually sparks interesting debate among owners of arrested players. Since the rules aren't clearly defined, we usually have three or four owners a year pleading their cases to Brennan and Steve as to why their player most deserves the Howe Award. Yes, it's tacky and juvenile, but so are Scott Boras and Donald Fehr and they're part of baseball too. Plus, its fun to hear a Grant Roberts owner debate Al Martin's as to why potheads are more grievous sinners than polygamists. It's like a year-long *Jerry Springer* episode without the midgets, mullets, fistfights, and interventions. Besides, how else could you find a legitimate reason to own Sidney Ponson?

Each league has its own set of traditions and awards. Anything that you can add that makes your league a little more unique adds to your league's lore and can help keep things fun for owners who might otherwise lose interest as their teams plummet in the standings.

Eighth Inning

Trading

Good drafting is probably the most important factor in building a winner, but trading is not far behind. Few teams are able to win a pennant without making at least a couple of good trades during the year. Whether you like to trade or not, you're probably not managing your roster effectively unless you make at least three or four trades every season. Here are some tips to help sharpen your trading skills.

Trading principles to live by

Here are a few guidelines you should consider when making trades with other owners.

Always be fair and ethical

It's important to be someone others can trust. Not only is being honest the right thing to do, but it endears you to other owners as well. If you establish a reputation of being an ethical owner, other teams won't hesitate to deal with you if you make an offer they like. Plus, if you're ever in a pennant race against another owner whose not-so-ethical, your fellow owners will be more inclined to help you instead of your competitor. I'm not suggesting that you don't seek an advantage in every trade (What would be the point of trading if you didn't?) but most owners know what a fair trade is and what's not.

As a general rule, don't pursue a deal that's grossly unfair, even if you're not the one who's offered it. If you're proposed a lopsided deal in your favor, you might casually try to throw in a player for another guy in return to even things out a bit. If you completely rip off another owner, chances are that your competitors will remind him of how badly he was robbed and portray you as one who can't be trusted. The next time you try to deal with that owner, he may tune you out completely. By making a more equitable deal, you can still get what you want and preserve that relationship for later.

Shady owners can ruin the fun for the entire league, and if you can't have fun this isn't a hobby worth having. Do your part to promote league harmony and be honest in your dealings.

Look to help your opponent

A rational owner must have a reason to make a trade. Before you make a trade offer to another owner, see how it would help him in the standings. Be ready to point out how the trade benefits him if he doesn't see it. Even if he doesn't make a deal, you've shown him how your offer was fair and he may be more receptive to your proposal next time.

Know your other owner

If he's a Yankees fan, offer him your Yankees players. If he likes power hitters, offer them in return for what you need. Pay particular attention to what each owner pursues in the draft, and make a note of which owners were the last to bid on players you acquired. If that owner made a competitive bid for one of your players, it's possible he'd love to acquire him in a trade.

Let the other guy make the first offer

I normally hint around that I'd like to make a deal and hope my opponent will make the first offer. Normally, I don't make the first proposal unless I'm in a hurry, or if two or three hints don't seem to get a response. I don't know how many times I've settled on a deal where I gave up less than I was willing to give because the other owner took less than I would have offered.

Don't make your best offer first, but don't insult the other owner either

If you're willing to trade a $30 hitter for a $30 pitcher, start by offering a $25 hitter for the same pitcher first. The other owner might accept your offer without your having to give up as much as you'd planned. If you make a lopsided offer right out of the gate, you're not likely to get anywhere.

Seek small advantages

Look to seek small advantages in your trades. If you make five trades and get a small advantage in each, you will have greatly improved your team without losing the trust of your fellow owners.

Buy low, sell high

Even great players sometimes perform at levels they can't possibly sustain over full seasons. If you own a player who can't possibly play better than he's playing at the present time and someone else values that player at his current performance level, trade him immediately. On the other hand, if you're offered a player who can't possibly be as bad as he's playing and you get him at a dime on the dollar, the odds are that trading for him will pay huge dividends.

Recognize the value of a superstar -- unless you're desperate, don't trade a good player for several lesser players

Decent players are plentiful but true superstars are rare. If you need to fill weak spots, it's tempting to trade a superstar for two or three guys who can help you more than what you have. You can almost always pick up ordinary players in a trade, but it's hard to get a Miguel Tejada or a Randy Johnson back once you've given him up. If you can trade a couple of decent players to a team that's desperate to fill some weak spots in return for a true superstar, make the deal. Leagues are won with superstars, and the more of them you have, the better your chance.

Always ask for the throw-in

Don't automatically accept a deal once it's to your liking. I've made a few deals where I would have accepted an owner's original proposal but said I needed "just a little more" to make a deal. It's usually something very minor like a late-round minor-league pick or an injured fifth-starter, but something that might help me down the road. If the other owner is dying to make a deal, you'll probably get a small bonus.

Making dump trades

The "dump trade," as it's commonly called, occurs when one team decides to throw in the towel for the current year and acquire talent that helps him in future seasons. Teams making dump trades should not expect full-value for their players. This is because they're essentially renting players to another owner for a few weeks or months while the dumping owner gets to keep his players for the next year or years. The value you receive in return for dumping depends on many factors, including the league's trading history, the relative scarcity or abundance of keepers in your league, and the number of owners who are looking to either build for the future or win now. As a general rule, the fewer good keepers available within the league, the less you should expect to receive when trading away quality players for future help.

If you're the person dumping, you should consider the future value of the players you're receiving in relation to their cost. If you're getting a player for the next two years who's going to be worth about $15 and he costs you $15, you're not really receiving value in return. The more a player is worth above his cost, the higher his value.

Consider this hypothetical trade offer in a typical 4x4 league (we'll suppose that the offer was made July 1):

Team A trades:

	Cost	Worth next year:	Yrs. left on contract
Craig Wilson	$5	$20	1
Ben Sheets	$10	$30	2

Estimated dollar value for this year: Sheets $30, Wilson $20; Total: $50

Team B trades:

Richard Hidalgo	$20	$20	1
Jim Edmonds	$30	-	-
Moises Alou	$15	$15	1
Russ Ortiz	$10	$15	1

Estimated dollar value for this year: Hidalgo $20, Edmonds $30, Alou $15, Ortiz $15; Total: $80

If I'm the dumping team (team B) and I'm offered this deal around mid-July, I'd do it in a heartbeat. I don't really care where I finish in the standings, and I'm getting Ben Sheets for the next two years at $20 above value the last two years -- a tremendous bargain, plus Craig Wilson at a very nice price for the next season. Edmonds can't be kept, so he doesn't concern me other than that I need to get maximum value for him in return and Alou and isn't going to be worth any more than what I'd have to pay him. I'm not losing anything for the future except a nicely-priced Ortiz, but I could live with that in return for what I'm getting.

If I'm the other owner, I would ask for at least another good player in return, and probably would not make the trade unless I was sure it was the best I could get and it virtually guaranteed me a title. Wilson-for-Hidalgo cancels out for the current season, but Hidalgo would give me nothing beyond this year. Ortiz isn't even in the same ballpark as Sheets in terms of value now, but Alou's addition cancels that out. So essentially, I would be renting Edmonds for half a season for the combined three-year futures of two bargain-priced players.

But the problem for the owner playing for now is this: other owners may be playing for this year as well. As soon as he mortgages his future, a competing owner could make a similar deal to negate everything he's just gained. It's awfully painful to trade away all your good keepers for the coming years and finish fourth. When making a trade like this, get all you can for your players and be relatively-certain that making the deal gives you a reasonable shot to win.

When evaluating dump trades, there are some other things to keep in mind:

1. The less time left in the season, the more talent the dumping team should give up in return. Yes, trading Johann Santana, Alfonso Soriano, and Manny Ramirez for Mark Teixeria looks lopsided on paper, but if it's August 31, you're in eleventh place, and Teixeria can be kept the next three years at $5, so what? Teixeira will probably be a $25-$30 player in most leagues for the foreseeable future, and if the former three aren't at reasonable prices for future seasons, they're of little value to you. Making that deal on April 30 is a different story.

2. Bargain keepers should have more value if fewer of them are available from one year to the next. In a league that uses 23-man rosters and most teams keep at least a half-dozen players or more at bargain prices from one year to the next, undervalued players should probably demand less in return. But in some leagues, the salary structure makes it nearly impossible for any one team to tie up substantially-undervalued players for a long time. Predictably, these bargains command more in return.

3. The players that the dumping team acquires should cost less than their value. A player who costs $21 but will only be worth $20 the following season isn't worth acquiring. If he's $19, he has little value. If he's $20, it's a wash.

4. Time horizons should be considered. For some reason, many owners don't consider the length of time for which they can sign a player. One year, I was chastised by an owner because I asked for Barry Bonds and John Smoltz (both at prices too expensive to keep the following year) in a mid-August deal in return for a $1 Marcus Giles. Giles could be kept for two more seasons and figured to be worth $20. The whole deal would have netted me about seven or eight homers, 10-12 RBI and runs scored, and about a dozen saves. But for some reason the other owner thought this proposal was heavily-stacked in my favor.

A $20 player who can be kept at $10 for the next two seasons is, of course, more valuable that the $20 player who can be kept at $10 for just one year. Consider contract time horizons in addition to salary issues.

5. Each league has its own opinions about what constitutes a fair deal. These norms can change over time, but sometimes you have to adapt to everyone else's standards of what makes a fair deal. The Giles proposal I described above is a great example – my offer was more than fair, but that particular league's owners largely ignore time horizons and salaries and look mostly at the names involved. I think this might change in time, but that season I had to give up a little more than what was reasonable in order to contend for a pennant, which didn't even work out in part due to Bonds' subsequent injury. As bad as that deal turned out to be, my other options at the time were even worse.

Furthermore, the money involved can influence how you and others view fairness in trading. If you play in a league where third place wins you $50, you might decide to play for the future and trade your players for dimes on the dollar and no one will really care. If your league's prize pot is worth several thousand dollars, though, it may be a different story. The increased cash makes a third-place finish more meaningful, and other owners are probably going to be less forgiving of any deal that appears "unbalanced," no matter what that deal means for your future.

Trading with unique owner types

Most of the battle of trading, of course, is persuading another owner that a particular deal is right for them. Owners come in all shapes and sizes, and each with their own set of peculiarities. Consummating a deal often takes much more than just a fair proposal when dealing with various human personalities. Some classes of owners present particular challenges -- here's how you should deal with these unique classes of potential trading partners:

The Rookie

The Rookie is often insecure with his knowledge of the game and often fears that potential trading partners are trying to rip him off. In most leagues, a few owners will make ridiculous trade proposals to The Rookie within the first weeks to take advantage of his naiveté. This may make him paranoid that every owner is a wolf in sheep's clothing.

Dealing with the rookie may take some time. Do not insult him with your first trade proposal because he may tune you out for good. When you're offering him a trade, take the time to explain how your offer meets his needs and why it's fair, and be patient if he doesn't bite the first few times. Once he's been in the league and learned what constitutes a fair deal, he'll be more likely to deal with you than with the guys who took advantage of him.

The Snake-Oil Salesman

There are owners in most leagues who rarely offer a fair trade. The Snake-Oil Salesman is often not a bad guy, but is a hyper-competitive person with an obsession for winning. In his quest for the path of least-resistance, he makes one trade offer after another to weaker owners, who eventually fall prey to his persistent pestering. The best way to deal with the Snake-Oil Salesman is to counteroffer his ridiculously-absurd proposals with an equally-insane one of your own. That shows him he's wasting his time with you until he can come up with a reasonable offer.

There is a point in time when you'll probably have to strike a deal out of necessity with a Snake-Oil Salesman. But no matter how desperate you become, never strike a lopsided deal with him. He's eventually going to alienate the fellow owners in your league, and once he's exhausted all his other options, he may come back to you with a fair offer. In some cases, he even may panic and offer a deal that's very much in your favor. Do not allow yourself to be trampled by him, and you may eventually gain a quality trading partner.

Mr. Status Quo

Some owners just don't like to deal. My brother Jon, owner of the Lee Press-On Nails, is this way -- he always feels that he's drafted a good team and sees no reason to make anything more than minimal roster moves. This has worked for him in most years but I think Jon is largely the exception to the rule. Have patience with Mr. Status Quo and don't expect your conversations to be very productive. Unless he needs to deal out of absolute necessity, it's generally a waste of your time to deal with him.

Navin R. Johnson

Navin Johnson (Steve Martin's idiot character in the 1979 comedy "The Jerk") will turn down a fair offer from you and then trade Randy Johnson to your competitor for Nate Cornejo. You have to spell everything out to Navin, who may or may not hear a word you say. Unlike Mr. Status Quo, you can't afford to cross Navin of your list of trading partners because your competitors won't. The GWPL had a Navin Johnson it's first year in existence; he traded Von Hayes (whose modern-day statistical equivalent is Torii Hunter) for two Cardinal benchwarmers named Steve Lake and Dane Iorg. When someone asked him why he made the trade, "Navin" (a Cardinal fan) said, "I didn't even know who Von Hayes was."

There are no really good ways to deal with Navin. Just keep making offers and hope he'll listen to reason every once in a while.

Mr. Know-It-All

Let Mr. Know-It-All do most of the talking and defer to his knowledge since this strokes his ego. If you let him speak long enough he may make you a favorable offer. These guys often don't know as much as they think they do and often write off decent players as "useless." Call Mr. Know-It-All when you need a roster-filler or two; he likely owns a couple of decent players that don't live up to his high standards.

Mr. Moody

There are usually owners in every league whose moods change as often as the direction of the wind. While I never advocate ripping anyone off, you should try to catch Mr. Moody the morning after his team goes three-for-37 and both his starters the previous night got shelled. Let him talk and find out who he's down on and see if he'll make a proposal; if not, make him a reasonable offer for someone he's down on that you might like. Your chances for making a good trade are rarely better than when you catch Mr. Moody after a bad day for his team.

Things can get especially interesting when the Snake-Oil Salesman meets with Mr. Moody. One year, our resident Snake-Oil Salesman caught Mr. Moody when he was about to go through a painful divorce and traded him spare parts and a box of rocks for John Smoltz and Reggie Sanders.

Smoltz won 24 games and the Cy Young Award that season, and Sanders hit 14 homers and stole 24 bases despite missing half the year. Guess who won the title that season?

Mr. Irrational

I promise I'm not making this up -- I once traded Scott Coolbaugh for Jeff Bagwell during each player's rookie season for reasons I still don't comprehend. Both players were unproven commodities but Bagwell seemed to have bigger upside at the time. This all happened because another owner tipped me off that Mr. Irrational "enjoyed hearing himself say the name 'Coolbaugh.'" Within ten minutes I made a phone call and had landed a future Hall of Famer for a player who ended his career with 432 major-league at-bats. Every now and then you'll encounter someone willing to make trades for no good reason. Seize the opportunity when it benefits you.

Mr. Ants-in-His-Pants

Mr. Ants-in-His-Pants is the antithesis of Mr. Status Quo. Mr. Ants-In-His-Pants feels the need to change his roster every ten minutes. Dave Schaubroeck, I'm talking about you. When I need to make a small move for any reason, I call Dave and we usually have a deal within a day or two, and we often deal on the spot. Dave turned his entire roster over three times last year. Many leagues have a Mr. Ants-In-His-Pants, and they're usually the easiest guys to deal with.

The Prospect Glutton

The Prospect Glutton gets cheap thrills from trying to find the next rookie before anyone else. He will fill his roster with guys who he thinks may be the next coming of Rogers Hornsby because he can't stand the thought of anyone else discovering these players first. The Prospect Glutton is often a smart owner, he just has an obsession with owning young players and it generally hinders him from finishing at the very top or the league. You can usually get more than fair value in dealing with the Prospect Glutton if you have anyone he's intent on owning.

Ninth Inning

The Minor Leagues

Note: This chapter is for those of you who have some sort of minor-league draft that's separate from your league's major-league draft. Even if you don't have a separate draft for prospects, you may consider reading the chapter anyway -- there are many tips that can help you evaluate young players.

Half the fun of playing fantasy baseball is spotting the next superstar before other owners in your league do. It's also an important part of a winning strategy. Paying less than full value for players is what helps you win your league, and undervalued players are usually youngsters in their first one-to-three years of major-league action.

The evaluation and ratings process for prospects has five steps:

1. Setting up a spreadsheet that includes column headings for all relevant data.

2. Entering player statistics.

3. Creating and entering formulas that reveal a player's abilities.

4. Making judgments about each player from past years -- is he improving, regressing, or staying the same?

5. Rating each player and assigning an estimated future value.

Evaluating and valuing minor-league talent

When evaluating the potential of a minor-league player, first consider the time horizon in which the player needs to produce. Since you may have a limited amount of time in which you may keep a player, you need someone who can contribute within the near future of his call-up. In other words, you don't care if someone will be a productive hitter in five years if your league's contract structure doesn't allow for you to keep a player that long. Yet surprisingly, many owners judge players more on a long-term basis than for the short-term. Unless your league has liberal rules allowing you to keep players on reserve for a few years, don't take many chances on players who are call-up candidates with no place to play.

Also, you should only judge players based on how they'll help you in the categories your league uses. I am amazed at how many experienced fantasy-leaguers draft according to some magazine's prospect list without regards to how the players they acquire would actually help their teams. Occasionally you'll see someone waste a high minor-league pick on a slick-fielding shortstop with a low average and zero power. Age and experience are also important factors; a 27 year-old hitter who rips AA pitching is almost never a prospect, while a 21 year-old who does the same generally is.

Once you've formed your opinion of players, you need to value each player for your league. If you wish, you could try to estimate future dollar values for that player, and that would certainly be a fine way to do things. I have used a 12-point evaluation scale for years. It's an arbitrary system, but it works well for me, and I'll share it with you here. Once I'm done with my ratings, I generally sort my spreadsheet according to those ratings to ensure that I've stayed consistent from one player to the next. Occasionally, I'll find that I was too generous on assigning points to a few players and too stingy with others. I'll then tweak the numbers a bit; after a few passes, I'll have ratings with which I'm comfortable.

When preparing for our league's minor league draft, I usually sort through Baseball Weekly's prospect issues, which usually come out in late fall to early winter. Sometimes I'll look at Baseball America's online ratings (which were formerly free, but you now have to subscribe to the magazine in order to get online access) to get a starting point for my list. John Benson's *Future Stars* is also a good source. If you can combine the lists from these two or three places, that's probably all the material you'll need to build a solid system of prospect ratings. If I need an online source to go get player stats from past years, I use TheBaseballCube.com.

Evaluating and rating hitters

If you play in a standard Rotisserie ™ league, you'll use the categories of batting average, stolen bases, RBI, and home runs. I'm assuming you play in a standard league, so we'll judge hitters according to these categories. However, you can easily make adjustments on your own if your league uses different categories. Here are the steps I take:

1. Create a spreadsheet with statistics headers. When rating hitters, I first create a spreadsheet and enter the following the following column headings (you'll want to use abbreviations or you'll not be able to print everything to one page, even if you use the "landscape" setting when you print):

- Team (abbreviated on my chart as "TM")
- Position ("POS")
- Age ("AGE")
- Year ("YR")
- What level(s) the player played at the each season ("LEV")
- Batting average ("AVG")
- At-bats ("AB")
- Home Runs ("HR")
- Walks ("BB")
- Strikeouts ("K")
- Stolen bases ("SB")
- On-base percentage ("OB%")
- Slugging percentage ("SL%")

I don't usually pay attention to RBI totals, which are not so much a function of a player's talent as they are his spot in the batting order and the talent around him.

2. Enter player data. How many players you rate, and how many years of stats you include, is up to you. You can generally look at a player and determine if he's draft-worthy in a few moments. I usually find about 75 players in each league who are worth evaluating. Anyway... take any player you feel is worth evaluating and enter, at a minimum, the above statistics from his past year. Save this list for a couple of years -- you might want to refer back to it later.

3. Create formulas to further evaluate players. Next, I create another set of column headings which I use to tell me crucial things about each player. These are:

- *Strikeouts to walks ratio* (abbreviated on my chart as "K/BB") -- the higher the number, the better. This number reveals important information about the player's strike-zone judgment. The formula is: **strikeouts / walks**
- *Walk rate* ("BB%") -- the more walks a batter is willing to take, the better. A high walk rate is indicative of a patient hitter. The walk-rate formula is: **(walks / (at-bats + walks)) x 100** (multiplying by 100 converts this number from a decimal to a percentage)
- *Strikeout rate* ("K%") -- the lower the strikeout frequency, the better. The formula: **(strikeouts / at-bats) x 100**
- *Home run rate* ("HR%") -- measures the hitter's home run power. The formula is: **(home runs / at-bats) x 100**
- *Stolen base frequency per 100 plate appearances* ("SBF") -- the number of bases per plate appearance, in percentage form, that a hitter steals. The formula for stolen-base frequency: **(stolen bases / (at-bats + walks)) x 100**

4. Making judgments about players. Once I've compiled this information for a hitter, I evaluate him on the following criteria:

A. How disciplined is he? I want to see a high on-base percentage with lots of walks and relatively-few strikeouts. The more a player exhibits these characteristics, the better his chances of making the majors and hitting for a high average once he's there. This is vitally important; if a player can't make contact or exhibit patience in the minors, he'll probably never stick in the big leagues. I prefer an on-base percentage of .370 or higher.

B. Can he hit for power, or does he show the potential to hit for power? High home run rates are obviously good. Sometimes younger players have developing power, which is why I include slugging percentage. If a player has a high slugging percentage but not a lot of homers, it's a sign that he may eventually hit more homers. I like to see a slugging percentage of .500 or higher.

C. Does he steal bases? This is not as important as the other factors, but if your league uses stolen bases, you'll want to know the player's track record. *Beware of guys who steal lots of bases but have low on-base percentages and don't hit for power.* They will never make it in the majors for a meaningful length of time, if at all.

Like RBI, steals aren't always a great gauge of ability because a player's steal total depends on who's hitting behind him and how often the manager lets him run. Still, if a player steals 40 bases, it's a pretty good indication he must be fast.

D. How old is the player? Once a hitter is 27, he's no longer much of a prospect. Every additional year of age means something; there is a big difference between a 21 year-old and a 25 year-old who put up identical stats at the same levels. If a player is 22 or younger and he's putting up great numbers in AA or AAA, take notice.

E. How does the player progress through the minors? Does he do well at all levels, or struggle upon promotion? Players are easier to project once they have significant experience at AA and AAA. Players who have not progressed past Rookie or "A" ball are harder to evaluate.

F. Are the player's statistics affected by the ballparks or the leagues in which he played? Some leagues, such as the Pacific Coast League, are notorious hitters' leagues. Be aware of the context in which the player accumulated his stats.

G. Is the player an injury risk? It helps if you can find data for players over several years so that you can determine whether the player is injury-prone.

H. Is the player versatile? Unless the player is a can't-miss prospect, he may need to switch positions to play in the majors. If he can't, his path to the majors could be blocked if there are quality major-leaguers or good minor-league prospects at his position.

I. Is he a good defensive player? Though defense doesn't count in most fantasy leagues, it can keep a good hitter out of the majors. Ask Jack Cust, whose career path to the majors was stalled well past the point his bat was ready because he fields baseballs as if they're porcupines.

J. Does he bat left-handed or right-handed, or switch-hit? Players who hit well from both sides of the plate are not as likely to platoon. If a player does platoon, the left-handed hitters see more playing time since there are more right-handed pitchers.

5. Consider major-league equivalents. A major-league equivalent is a statistical projection of what a player would likely do at the major-league level based on his stats, which are adjusted for his age and the minor leagues in which he's played. These are available many places, including *The Forecaster.*

6. Rate players on a 12-point scale. Once I have a player's vital statistics and I've formed an opinion of him, I evaluate him on a twelve-point system as described below. You may wish to set up your system differently, but I find this works well for the typical 23-player, $260 salary-cap league.

A. Potential (up to five points) Potential is estimated as shown below. You may wish to change the dollar values if your salary structure is vastly different from the standard 23-team, $260 cap, but if not, this one's always worked fine for me:

- **5 points**: If this player were given a chance to play full-time in the majors with an average organization and in an average ballpark, he has the talent to be worth $30 or more within three years of his promotion to the majors.

- **4.5 points**: Same conditions as above, the player could be worth $25-29

- **4 points:** The player could be worth $20-24

- **3.5 Points:** $15-19

- **3 points:** $10-14

- **2.5 Points:** $5-10

If a player's not a 2.5 or higher, I don't bother assigning him a rating.

This begs the question of how to know what a player might be worth. I suggest projecting stats for each prospect, then seeing which major-league players they most resemble statistically and projecting the prospect's dollar value according to your comparisons.

B. Risk (up to five points). Risk is the next element of the rating system. It is similar to opportunity in that it considers a player's skill, but the idea of risk assessment is to look at flaws that could keep him from reaching his potential. If, at the minor-league level, a player doesn't walk or strikes out too much, it doesn't matter how much power he has because he probably won't be able to make contact at the major-league level. Age, experience, and injury risk are also factors. I usually begin to downgrade a player after his 24th birthday if he's not played at least at the AA level, or if he struggles consistently upon being promoted to a new level. I use the following criteria as guidelines, but not absolutes -- in other words, I am free to bend my rules a bit if I feel common sense dictates that I should do so.

Ratings are determined by the criteria that follow:

- **5 points:** No older than 23, has performed well at no less than AA for a year, no major holes in the player's game. This player can hit for big power, take a walk, and doesn't strike out too often. There is rarely a player that I'd consider rating a five.

- **4.5 points:** No older than 24, no major holes in his skills and has either performed well for at least a couple months at AA or is described by everyone as a "can't miss" guy for players without AA experience.

- **4 points:** No older than 25; if the player is 25, he must have no major weaknesses. If the player is younger, he must still have acceptable strikeout and walk numbers (nothing worse than two strikeouts per walk) but can have one flaw in his game (single-digit steals or sub-15 home runs per year power). I usually rate the Mark McGwire/Adam Dunn-type hitter a "four" -- these hitters may strike out a lot, but also take a lot of walks and have high on-base percentages to compliment big power.

- **3.5 points:** An OK prospect; usually a guy who either steals a lot of bases and has no power or a guy who might have moderate speed and/or power, but no one outstanding aspect to his game. Guys with major power who have strikeout-to-walk ratios of worse than 2:1 usually reside here.

- **3.0 points:** These are generally players with tremendous speed but horrible on-base percentages, or guys with major power and speed who strike out a lot and don't walk much.

- **2.5 points:** Guys with serious power who strike out at least four times for every walk they take (think Russell Branyan). These players make noise when they connect but they connect so infrequently at the minor-league level that their chances of being successful major-leaguers are slim. Players with serious injury problems may fit here as well.

Like potential ratings, chance ratings are very subjective. Generally, the more things that work against a player and the more serious those things are, the further he falls. I've tried to make this into an objective system that assigns points for age, experience, strikeout rates, and other things, but it didn't work as well as looking at a player's total package and then assigning the rating.

The key is to be consistent in your ratings. It helps if you can put all your hitters into one spreadsheet and compare their numbers; one four-point player should look similar to another. If you've got a 22 year-old with good power and a .75 K/BB ratio rated a "three" while other similar prospects are "fours" you'll be able to pick these things out and make adjustments once you've sorted all players by their numerical ratings. You'll get a good feel for how to rate players once you've evaluated a few dozen prospects.

C. Opportunity. Opportunity composes the last part of the rating system. It is worth two points in the rating system, and is calculated as follows.

- **2 points:** Everything is in the player's favor. The player plays in a hitter's park like Coors Field or Yankee Stadium (if he's a lefty), has no competition at his position from within his team's farm system, and should easily beat out the regular at his position on his major-league team upon promotion. I very rarely rate a player a two.

- **1.5 points:** Conditions are very favorable for this player. By the time he is promoted to the majors, he should have a regular job and should play in a decent park. He has little to no competition from other organizational prospects in his system from players close to his skill level and no one at his position that is better than he is.

- **1 point:** This is generally the default rating. These are players who may have another prospect at the same position at or near their performance levels, and play in decent, but not great, hitters parks. This player could stand a chance of beating out the ML regular once they reach the majors.

- **0.5 points:** Usually a player with stiff competition from within his own system, or a player with a very good major-league prospect who won't be traded any time soon in front of him. This could be a very good player with a pathetic team like the Pirates, who can't distinguish a good ballplayer from a tuna fish sandwich, so the player may not get the chance he deserves.

- **0 points:** Players in unenviable situations. A "zero" may be a decent player who, for whatever reason, has virtually no chance of reaching the majors with his current team, and isn't versatile enough to stand a position switch. Top-level prospects would probably not be rated zeros because they're good enough ballplayers to overcome most any circumstance, whether it be a defensive deficiency or the misfortune of being in the wrong organization.

Let me walk you through a few prospects to show you how I use this system:

Jason Stokes, 1B, Florida (stats below)

TM	POS	AGE	YR	LEV	AVG	AB	HR	BB	K	SB	OBP	SLG	K/BB	BB%	K%	HR%	SBF
FL	1B	19	'01	A	231	130	6	11	48	0	301	400	4.4	7.8	36.9	2.6	0.0
		20	'02	A	341	349	27	47	96	1	425	641	2.0	11.9	27.5	7.9	0.3
		21	'03	A	258	462	17	36	135	6	312	448	3.8	7.2	29.2	6.6	1.2

1. Potential: Stokes, by all accounts, has big-time power potential. He's got a large frame and has hit for power since day one, and had very impressive power numbers at age 20. He hasn't advanced past high "A" ball yet, but he's also at an age where most players have not developed significant power, either. He's not going to be a .300 hitter immediately or steal many bases, but I could see him hitting .270 with 25-30 homers and 90-100 RBI within three years of a major-league promotion. In my league, that would make him a $20-24 hitter. *Rating: 4*

2. Risk: Stokes needs to learn to make better contact and take a few walks, but there have been many good power hitters that performed similarly at that age. However, it should be noted that he battled a wrist injury all of 2003 which adversely affected his game, and with a 2.0 K/BB ratio when he was healthy, there's certainly room for hope. You have to give him credit for dominating a league at such an early age, but also downgrade him a bit since he's proven nothing above "A" ball. He's got plenty of time to develop, and with his power, he'll get a shot at the majors. *Rating: 3.5*

3. Opportunity: Stokes plays for the Marlins organization, who just acquired Hee-Seop Choi before the '04 season began (Choi's since been traded to LA, but since I'm looking at him as if 2004 hadn't begun, I'll ignore that.). Therefore, there's no obvious spot for him to play, but I'll bet they'll move one of the two to the outfield by the time he's ready, which should be two or three years. Florida's park is not a friend to hitters, but it's not LA or San Francisco, either. *Rating: 1.5*

Stokes' total rating: 9

Josh Barfield, 2B, San Diego

TM	POS	AGE	YR	LEV	AVG	AB	HR	BB	K	SB	OBP	SLG	K/BB	BB%	K%	HR%	SBF
SD	2B	18	'01	R	310	277	4	12	54	16		437	4.5	4.2	19.5	1.3	5.5
		19	'02	A	87	23	0	1	4	0	87	120	4.0	4.2	17.4	0.0	0.0
		19	'02	A	306	536	8	26	105	26	340	403	4.0	4.6	19.6	2.6	4.6
		20	'03	A	337	549	16	50	122	16	389	530	2.4	8.3	22.2	4.7	2.7

1. Potential: Like Stokes, Barfield has had nice power numbers at an early age, though not quite on par with the Marlins' slugger. However, Barfield has displayed decent speed on the base paths and has hit for an excellent average. The on-base percentages are coming along nicely, and he appears to be learning to take a few walks. His slugging percentage numbers reflect developing power; he's hit for average and could add double-digit steals, and could settle into being a .290, 20-homer, 15-steal, 70 RBI-type player, giving him a dollar value of around $20 in my league. *Rating: 4*

2. Risk: He's still young and has those strikeout numbers working against him, but he was San Diego's Minor League Player of the Year and has great bloodlines -- his father, Jesse, was a major-league standout for several years. He's a second baseman who hits like an outfielder, which further helps his chances. However, there's no track record beyond A-ball and unlike Stokes, has not gotten his K/BB ratio below two. *Rating: 3*

3. *Opportunity:* Mark Loretta's no spring chicken, so Barfield will get his shot in a couple of years. However, Petco Park appears to be an awful place for hitters, and that eats into his rating just a bit. *Rating: 1*

Barfield's total rating: 8

J.J. Hardy, SS, Milwaukee

TM	POS	AGE	YR	LEV	AVG	AB	HR	BB	K	SB	OBP	SLG	K/BB	BB%	K%	HR%	SBF
MIL	SS	19	'01	R	250	20	0	1	2	0		450	2.0	4.8	10.0	0.0	0.0
		19	'01	R	248	125	2	15	12	1		336	0.8	10.7	9.6	0.8	0.7
		20	'02	A	293	335	6	19	38	9	327	409	2.0	5.4	11.3	2.0	2.5
		20	'02	AA	228	145	1	9	19	1	269	297	2.1	5.8	13.1	0.4	0.6
		21	'03	AA	279	416	12	58	54	6	368	428	0.9	12.2	13.0	4.3	1.3

1. *Potential:* Before 2003, there wasn't a lot to be excited about from a fantasy standpoint -- Hardy didn't hit for average or much power, nor did he really get on base. But as young players often do, Hardy improved significantly in his 2003 AA follow-up, displaying more power and an excellent strikeout-to-walk ratio. Hardy looks as if he could be a decent offensive player, but nothing to get really excited about. He's probably a $7-8 player if he plays every day, maybe a little more if he continues to improve as he did in 2003. *Rating: 2.5*

2. *Risk:* Hardy's a solid fielder and has been anointed the Brewers' shortstop of the future, so a spot should be waiting. He's not consistently put up any special numbers offensively, but the strikeout-to-walk ratios are very good, and he has proven himself at AA, and did so at a young age. He probably won't hit for a ton of power, but that rarely keeps a shortstop out of the majors if he can field his position well, and it appears that he can. *Rating: 3.5*

3. *Chance:* There's no irreplaceable player in Milwaukee holding down shortstop, and Hardy appears to be their guy. He'll play in a great hitter's park, which helps his chances of success. *Rating: 1.5*

Hardy's total rating: 7.5

Evaluating and rating the pitchers

As with hitters, your system should be set up along the lines of your league's categories. In the league I will use here, those categories are wins, saves, strikeouts, and ERA.

Pitchers who are going to succeed at the big-league level should generally exhibit the following characteristics in the minor leagues: at least 7.5 strikeouts per nine innings, walk levels below four walks per nine, a strikeout-to-walk ratio of at least 2:1, and allow no more than one home run allowed per nine innings. Prospects should be able to perform well at every level, and a player should at least be in AA by the time he's 24. Size helps, though it's not a crucial factor. Bigger guys are usually more durable and ML teams seem more prone to promote them than smaller players, everything else being equal.

I don't pay much attention to scouting reports that talk about how great a pitcher's "stuff" is unless he fits most of the above criteria. If a player has great stuff, it should show in his strikeout numbers. Also, I tend to downgrade guys with big strikeout numbers who walk five guys or more per nine innings -- if you can't find the plate, big-league hitters are not going to swing. I also don't pay much attention to won-loss records or ERA. There are a lot of guys with good ERA's and records who won't ever sniff the majors. However, there are players like Kerry Wood who may not have the greatest minor-league ERA's or records but have the stuff to succeed. Also, don't go after minor-league closers. These guys almost never close for major-league teams, even later in their careers.

I tend to be a bit stingier with pitching point ratings. Pitchers are usually more subject to injuries and their performance fluctuates more than hitters, in general. There are a few can't-miss guys like Josh Beckett, but even some of these players might take some pretty bizarre career paths, like Rick Ankiel did. I won't try to prove it, but there are probably three or four legitimate "can't-miss" hitters like an Adam Dunn or Albert Pujols for every "can't miss" pitching prospect.

1. Create a spreadsheet. When rating pitchers, I enter the following column headings on my pitching spreadsheet:

- Team (abbreviated "TM")
- Throws ("T") -- this is to indicate whether a player is left or right-handed
- Age ("AGE")
- Innings pitched ("IP")

- Hits allowed ("H")
- Home runs allowed ("HR")
- Walks allowed ("BB")
- Strikeouts ("K")

2. Enter player data. Consult your prospect lists and enter the stats for as many players as you wish to evaluate.

3. Create formulas to further evaluate players. Now, create more columns to the right of these data, and enter formulas to find key information about these prospects. The formulas are:

- *Strikeouts-to-walks ratio* (abbreviated on my chart as "K/BB") -- the higher the number, the better. This is a great gauge of both control and effectiveness. The formula is **strikeouts / walks.**
- *Strikeouts per nine innings* ("K/9") -- this measures a pitcher's dominance over hitters. The formula: **(strikeouts / innings pitched) x 9**
- *Walks per nine innings* ("BB/9") -- measures a pitcher's control. The formula: **(walks / innings pitched) x 9**
- *Home runs allowed per nine innings ("HR/9")* -- tells you whether the pitcher is prone to giving up the long ball. The formula: **(home runs / innings pitched) x 9**
- *Hits per nine innings* ("H/9") -- tells you the frequency with which a pitcher allows hits. The formula for this is **(hits / innings pitched) x 9**

4. Making judgments about players. After compiling the data for pitchers, I ask the following questions:

A. Does the pitcher have control of his pitches? Generally speaking, you want someone who walks fewer than four guys per nine innings, and has a strikeout-to-walk ratio of at least two-to-one. If the pitcher can't exhibit control in the minor leagues, he can't be expected to do this in the majors.

B. Is he dominant? Does he strike out 7.5 or more guys per nine innings? Unless a player has exceptional control, don't consider him unless he can achieve this mark. Also, make adjustments for players as they move up the minor-league ranks. A player who strikes out nine guys per nine innings in AAA is probably a prospect, but if he's 24 and does this in A-ball, he's probably not a prospect.

C. Is he hittable? Ideally, the player should give up less than one home run per nine innings, and fewer than eight hits per nine innings. Be more concerned with the home run figure than the hit figure.

D. How big is he? This is not as important as the other questions, but generally speaking, big-league teams are enamored with big guys; the thinking is, if a player is large, he's going to be more durable. Conversely, the little guys sometimes get overlooked unless they've got outstanding stuff (Billy Wagner and Roy Oswalt are two little guys who did just fine). When choosing between two guys with equal ability, take the big guy.

E. Is he left-handed or right-handed? Big-league clubs love lefties, so when everything else is equal, take the lefty.

F. How old is he? I have a greater age tolerance for pitchers than hitters. There are often decent pitchers who don't crack the majors until they're 26-28. Although in choosing between two pitchers with the same ability, I'd generally choose the younger guy. However, one warning -- you don't see many guys who are genuinely ready for the majors before 23 or 24, and pitchers usually don't peak until they're around 30. So, even if a player has been very successful at all levels and he's only 20 or 21, be cautious. Players this young stand a good chance of being bombed once they reach the majors.

G. Is the pitcher an injury risk? Young pitchers are more susceptible to arm injuries. Be aware of a player's past injury history, and watch out for guys who throw more than 180 innings per season in their teens and early-20's. Young pitchers often get hurt as a result of throwing lots of pitches at a young age.

5. Rating pitchers on a twelve-point scale. The process is similar to what we did with hitters:

A. Potential. The potential scale for pitchers is the same as for hitters.

B. Risk. Pitchers as a whole are riskier than hitters. Risk points are given as follows:

- **5 points:** A "can't-miss" prospect. No older than 22; has shown dominance at AA or above, has awesome strikeout numbers (at least 10.5 K's per nine innings), great control (less than 2.5 walks per game), and keeps the ball in the park. Truthfully, no pitcher should probably ever be rated a five because of the injury risk, but it's your choice if you feel the rating is justified.

- **4.5 points:** Same as above, but is no more than 23 years old.

- **4 points:** A dominant player who is 24-25, or a player who is younger than 24 but may be a little wild (over 3.5 walks per nine) or gives up a home run or more per nine innings. Could also be a player with outstanding control but not quite a dominant pitcher (less than 7.5 K's/9) or a dominant pitcher with minor control issues or an injury history.

- **3.5 points:** A solid prospect: either a great strikeout pitcher who's wild or a good control pitcher who's not dominant. Or, this could be an older player – perhaps as old as 26 – who puts up outstanding number in the upper minors.

- **3 points:** A player with good, but not great numbers or a player who's an extreme control pitcher with "K" numbers less than six per nine innings. Or, this could be a player with a 2:1 K/BB ratio but walks five or more hitters per nine.

- **2.5 points:** A player with a good skill, but enough deficiencies that will probably prevent him from reaching the majors.

- **2.0 and below:** Don't bother.

C. Opportunity. Opportunity is calculated as follows:

- **2 points:** The player is good enough to immediately step into his team's rotation and produce. There are no prospects in the organization that will get a shot ahead of him. He plays in a great pitcher's park like LA or Oakland.

- **1.5 points:** The same qualities apply as in the above case, except the pitcher plays in a decent or neutral pitching park.

- **1 point:** A good player facing some competition that makes his future uncertain, and who plays in a decent park, or a player without steep competition who pitches in a poor park like Milwaukee or Houston. Most pitchers qualify as a "one."

- **0.5 points:** A player facing stiff competition who plays in a poor park.

- **0 points:** Most Colorado pitchers.

Here's how I'd rate these selected pitchers:

Cole Hamels, LHP, Philadelphia

TM	TH	AGE	YR	LEV	IP	H	HR	BB	K	K/BB	K/9	BB/9	HR/9	H/9
PHI	L	20	'03	A	74.67	32	0	25	115	4.6	13.9	3.0	0.0	3.9
		20	'03	A	26.33	29	0	14	32	2.3	10.9	4.8	0.0	9.9

1. Potential: Hamels' numbers in his first pro season were off-the-charts. His numbers dipped a little bit upon his promotion to high-A ball, but it's not as if 10.9 strikeouts per nine innings are anything to sneeze at. Plus, he didn't allow a home run all season. There's some work to do on that control, but he looks every bit like a guy that could win 17-18 games with a great ERA and ratio in the near future. *Rating: 4*

2. Risk: Because of Hamels' lack of a track record, we don't really know how he'll progress through the system and respond as the competition gets tougher. His control numbers aren't perfect either and he's had a couple of arm injuries (a broken humerus, and another non-baseball related arm injury that he later aggravated) that are cause for some concern. Anyone this good will certainly get a chance, but the control issues, lack of experience, and injury history suggest he's far from a sure thing. *Rating: 4*

3. Opportunity: There's little question that Hamels will have a chance to be a top-of-the-rotation pitcher if he stays healthy, and with Philadelphia's current roster talent, have a chance to be a big winner as well. I don't know what kind of park Philly's new field is, so I'll not attempt a guess. *Rating: 1.5*

Hamels' total rating: 9.5

Dan Meyer, LHP, Atlanta

TM	TH	AGE	YR	LEV	IP	H	HR	BB	K	K/BB	K/9	BB/9	HR/9	H/9
ATL	L	21	'02	R	65.67	47	4	18	77	4.3	10.6	2.5	0.5	6.4
		22	'03	A	81.67	76	6	15	95	6.3	10.5	1.7	0.7	8.4
		22	'03	A	78.33	69	7	17	63	3.7	7.2	2.0	0.8	7.9

1. Potential: Meyer pitched brilliantly in his rookie ball debut, and then had an equally-impressive follow-up among his promotion to A-ball. Once sent to A-ball, Meyer pitched well but the dominance he exhibited in the previous two stops had significantly diminished. Still, Meyer has shown outstanding control so far and some of the drop-off upon his promotion might be attributed to the toll of an unprecedented number of innings on a 22-year old arm. At this point, though, there's no reason to think he couldn't pitch well at the ML level. *Rating: 3.5*

2. Risk: There is a significant amount of risk involved with any young pitcher with no experience beyond A-ball, but Meyer's control has to temper some of that risk just a bit. Still, I'll have to see Meyer succeed at AA or higher -- or have a completely dominating year like Hamels had -- before I'll give him a more favorable risk rating. *Rating: 3*

3. Opportunity: Meyer looks like the best pitching prospect in Atlanta's system, and with the Braves' rotation a far cry from the days of Maddux/Glavine/Smoltz, he'll get a shot one day. Once he gets there, he plays in a nice pitcher's park, too. *Rating: 1.5*

Meyer's total rating: 8

Brandon Claussen, LHP, Cincinnati

TM	TH	AGE	YR	LEV	IP	H	HR	BB	K	K/BB	K/9	BB/9	HR/9	H/9
CIN	L	20	'99	R	11.33	7		2	16	8.0	12.7	1.6	0.0	5.6
		20	'99	A	6	8		7	2	0.3	3.0	10.5	0.0	12.0
		20	'99	A	72	70		12	89	7.4	11.1	1.5	0.0	8.8
		21	'00	A	97.33	91		44	96	2.2	8.9	4.1	0.0	8.4
		21	'00	A	51.66	49		17	44	2.6	7.7	3.0	0.0	8.5
		22	'01	A	56	47	2	13	69	5.3	11.1	2.1	0.3	7.6
		22	'01	AA	131	101	6	55	151	2.7	10.4	3.8	0.4	6.9
		24	'03	A	22	16	0	3	26	8.7	10.6	1.2	0.0	6.5
		24	'03	AAA	15	17	3	6	16	2.7	9.6	3.6	1.8	10.2
		24	'03	AAA	68.67	53	4	18	39	2.2	5.1	2.4	0.5	6.9
		24	'03	ML	6.33	8	1	1	5	5.0	7.1	1.4	1.4	11.4

1. Potential: Claussen led the minors in strikeouts at age 22 before suffering an arm injury that sidelined him for a year. He made a respectable comeback two years later and lost a little bit of his dominance, but lost nothing (and may have actually improved) his control. Knowing that he's once been a dominant pitcher and that he had a respectable return at 24, there's no reason to believe that Claussen couldn't become a good major-league pitcher if his health permits. *Rating: 3.5*

2. Risk: There's obviously an injury risk here; however, there's little else to be concerned about. Claussen has pitched reasonably-well at all levels, including a cup of coffee in the majors. Injuries usually take a couple of years to recover from, and he pitched well in his first year back. The future looks as if it could be bright, but you do have to discount him a bit because of his history. *Rating: 3.5*

3. Opportunity: Cincinnati has no top-quality pitchers at the big-league level, and Claussen is likely as talented as anyone in the organization. A rotation spot awaits him soon, but when he gets there, he'll be pitching in a hitter-friendly park. *Rating: 1*

Claussen's total rating: 8

Assessing the value of a minor-league player in trades

Some leagues allow you to trade minor-league prospects for major-league players. While these trades are a bit difficult to size up because you're comparing apples to oranges, you should keep the following things in mind when considering these kinds of deals:

1. Consider your league's salary and contract structure. If your league allows you to lock up minor-leaguers for several years at cheap salaries, top prospects become more valuable.

2. Don't lose sight of the risk involved. There are no guarantees even among major-league players, which makes minor-leaguers all-the-more more risky. No matter how much you believe someone is a "can't-miss" prospect, you should still de-value him a bit in comparison with major-leaguers just because he's not proven anything in The Show.

3. Factor in your situation. If you're in a pennant race this season and your roster is stocked with quality players, having one of your stud prospects promoted to the major leagues may not be a good thing if you have to put him on your active roster or lose him. If this happens to you, start looking for a trade partner who's not playing for this season.

Extra Innings

Acknowledgements

I owe a large debt of gratitude to several people for their help and encouragement in publishing this book. First of all, I would like to give a huge thank you to Brennan McGehee and the owners of the Ed Whitson League. Brennan provided dozens of hours of great editorial suggestions and tremendous ideas on how to improve this book. Brennan is also responsible for getting the manuscript in the hands of several of the Whitson League's owners, including Rob Hootselle and others. Thank you guys for your suggestions as well.

Thank you to the owners of the Cool Papa Bell League. My CPBL experience has taught me many things, and some CPBL owners were the inspiration for examples in this book. I would like to give special thanks to Todd Loyd, my co-owner and good friend in the CPBL, who introduced me to my first "mixed league."

As for the GWPL, so many of you deserve a mention that it's hard to know where to begin. Thank you to my brothers, Jon and Jeff Lee, for their support and content suggestions over the past four years. A couple more GWPL, Dave Schaubroeck and Bart Walker, deserve special mention, too. They are great competitors as well as special friends.

Several former GWPL owners also left a profound impact on my baseball-related thinking, especially Randy Fletcher and Tommy Phelps, who are two of the shrewdest owners I've ever played against. I learned as much from Randy and Tommy about how to win as I have anyone.

Thanks to Tim Murphy at Author House for his help over the past year. Tim was instrumental in helping me meet publishing deadlines and generously gave advice regarding marketing strategy. I could not have published the book in time for the 2005 season without his help.

Mike Rapp and his company, GearInc., designed the fantastic cover of this book. I knew that when I challenged Mike with the task of putting a suitable face on my work, he'd come up with something that blew me away. Mike is a world-class designer and he can be contacted at his firm in Franklin, Tennessee through the E-mail address <u>mike@gearinc.net</u>.

I wanted a professional-looking website to accompany this book, and with Michael Utley's help, I got it. Check out my site at baseballhandbook. com and see what Mike's done. I highly recommend him if you're thinking of producing a high-quality website.

Finally, the ultimate debt of gratitude goes to my wife, Lisa Lee. I began the groundwork for this book during our engagement and spent a good part of the first three years of our marriage hammering away at my manuscript until it felt "right." She spent a lot of lonely nights and weekends when I was around in body but not in mind, and exhibited more patience and support than I probably deserved. I thank her for making my hopes and dreams with this book hers as well.

ORDERING INFORMATION

If you'd like to purchase additional copies of the book, please visit our website at www.baseballhandbook.com. If you need information on bulk ordering, please visit www.authorhouse.com or call 888-280-7715.

To contact the author, please E-mail Chris Lee at chris@baseballhandbook.com.

About the Author

Chris Lee has played fantasy baseball for 19 years, winning several league titles in the process. Chris has both undergraduate and graduate degrees in business administration and currently teaches undergraduate economics at O'More College of Design in Franklin, Tennessee, where he also serves as Dean of Enrollment. Chris is the Senior Editor and Publisher of VandySports.com, the exclusive Vanderbilt site on the Rivals.com network, has also written for *Southeastern Football Saturdays* and ESPN. com's *Campus Insider*, and has done radio work as a college sports and baseball analyst for stations in South Carolina and Tennessee. He lives in Nashville, Tennessee with his wife, Lisa.

Breinigsville, PA USA
23 December 2009
229744BV00003B/84/A